America THE *Beautiful*

NORTH CAROLINA

NORA CAMPBELL

DAN LIEBMAN Series Editor

To Scott + Karen Kyle
on your visit to N.C.
Susan Guthrie

FIREFLY BOOKS

A Firefly Book

Published by Firefly Books Ltd. 2009

First printing

Publisher Cataloging-in-Publication Data (U.S.)

Campbell, Nora.
North Carolina / Nora Campbell.
[ ] p. : col. photos. ; cm. America the beautiful series.
Summary: A book of captioned photographs that showcase the natural wonders, dynamic cities, celebrated history and array of activities of North Carolina.
ISBN-13: 978-1-55407-547-8
ISBN-10: 1-55407-547-5
1. North Carolina – Pictorial works. I. Title. II. America the beautiful.
975.6 dc22 F255.C367 2009

Library and Archives Canada Cataloguing in Publication

North Carolina / [captions written by] Nora Campbell.
(America the beautiful)
ISBN-13: 978-1-55407-547-8
ISBN-10: 1-55407-5475
1. North Carolina--Pictorial works. I. Campbell, Nora II. Series: America the beautiful (Richmond Hill, Ont.)
F255.N67 2009 975.6'0440222 C2009-901480-7

Published in the United States by
Firefly Books (U.S.) Inc.
P.O. Box 1338, Ellicott Station
Buffalo, New York 14205

Published in Canada by
Firefly Books Ltd.
66 Leek Crescent
Richmond Hill, Ontario L4B 1H1

Cover and interior design: Kimberley Young

Printed in China

The publisher gratefully acknowledges the financial support for our publishing program by the Government of Canada through the Book Publishing Industry Development Program.

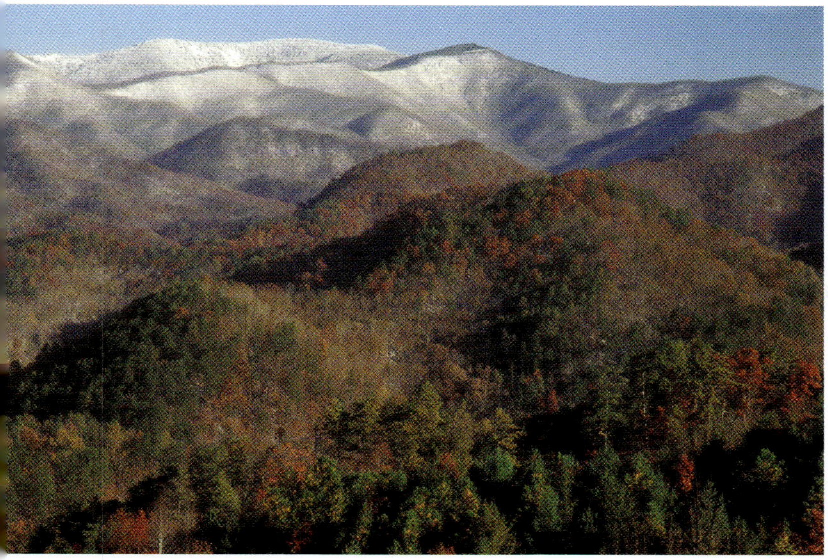

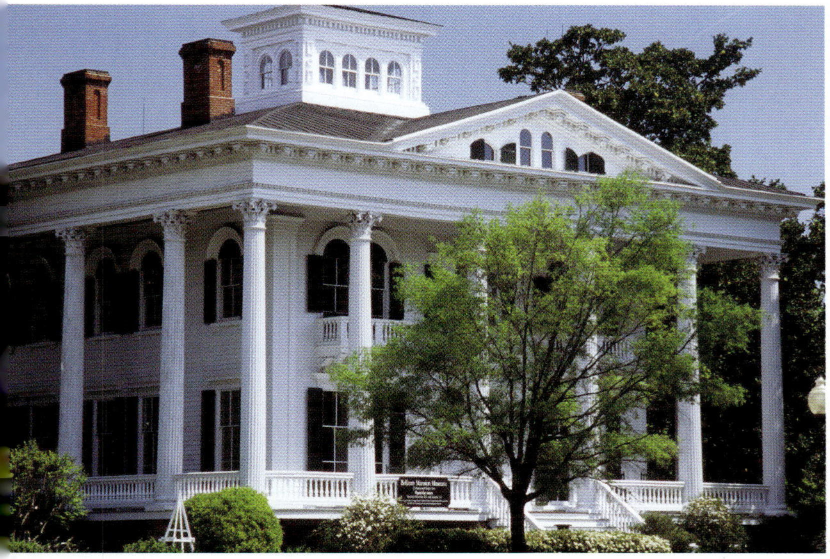

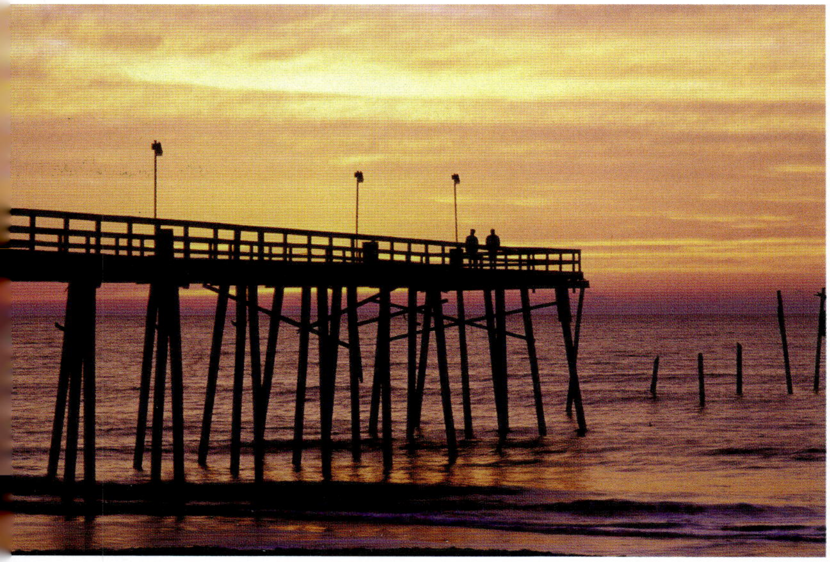

LIKE A GEM with many facets, North Carolina presents a sparkling diversity of natural wonders, dynamic cities, a celebrated history and a vast array of sport and cultural activities.

The beauty of this state surrounds travelers at every turn. The northwest region offers many scenic drives through the majestic Smoky Mountains. The roads are engineering feats in themselves, designed not only to allow the best vantage points for viewing, but also to protect the natural habitats and landscapes. North Carolina boasts four national forests, thick with more species of trees than there are in all of Europe. Many hiking and mountain biking trails wander through these vast protected areas and offer an excellent chance to see an amazing diversity of plant and animal life.

But no less spectacular is the coastal region with its seemingly endless miles of white sandy beaches and undulating sand dunes. Protecting the coastline from the stormy Atlantic is the chain of barrier islands called the Outer Banks.

Meanwhile, the central geographic region reflects the modern spirit of the state. Dazzling skyscrapers rise up from the major metropolitan areas, including Charlotte and Raleigh. Renowned museums, aquariums, zoos and historic buildings are popular attractions. Superb examples of modern architecture illustrate the potential of North Carolina, while the many exquisite examples of colonial structures serve as reminders of the state's historic settlement and proud heritage.

From the splendor of its thriving cities and the charm of its quaint villages to its magnificent natural wonders, the state offers an abundance of treasures. We hope you'll enjoy them as you travel the pages of *America the Beautiful – North Carolina.*

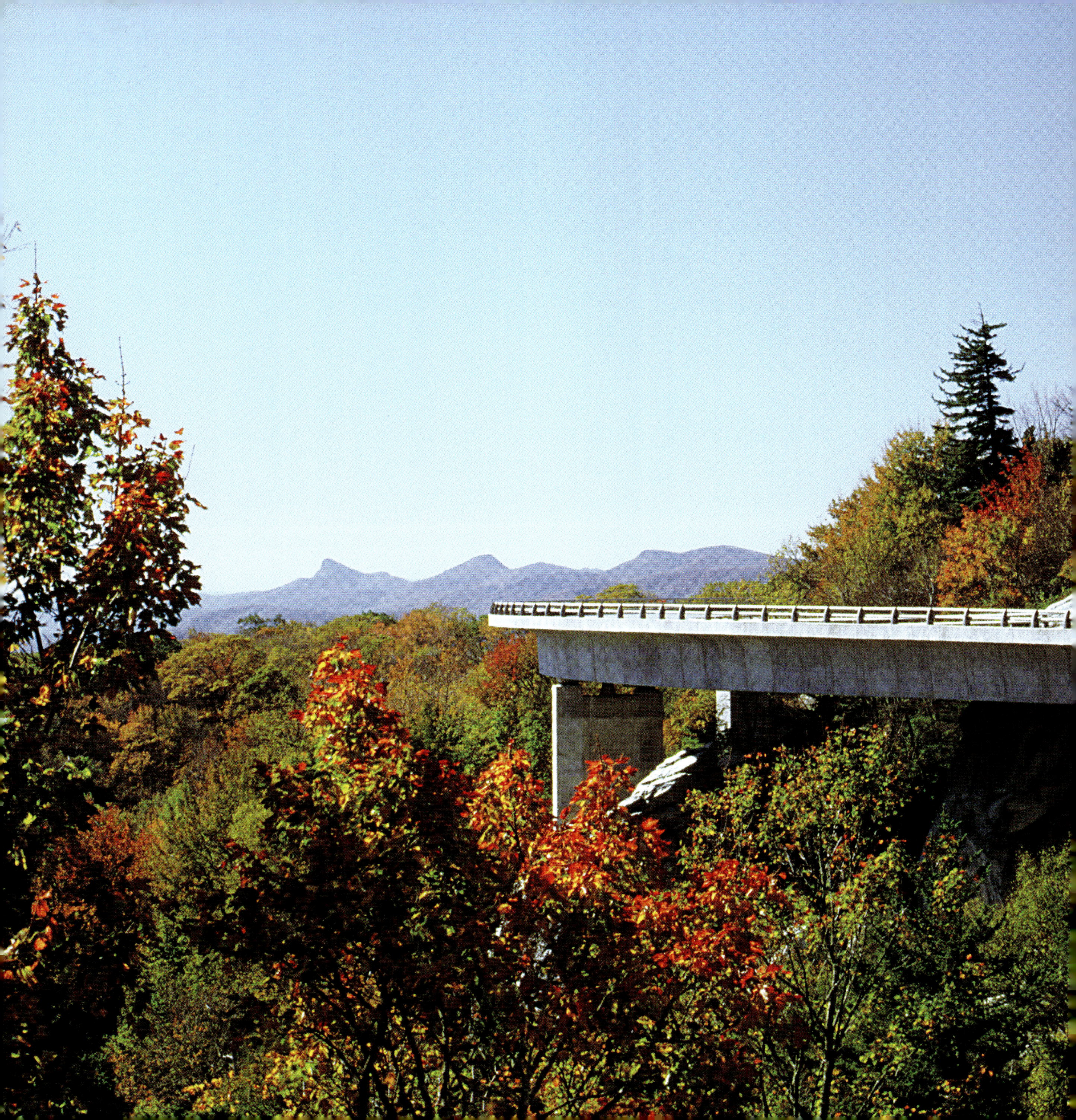

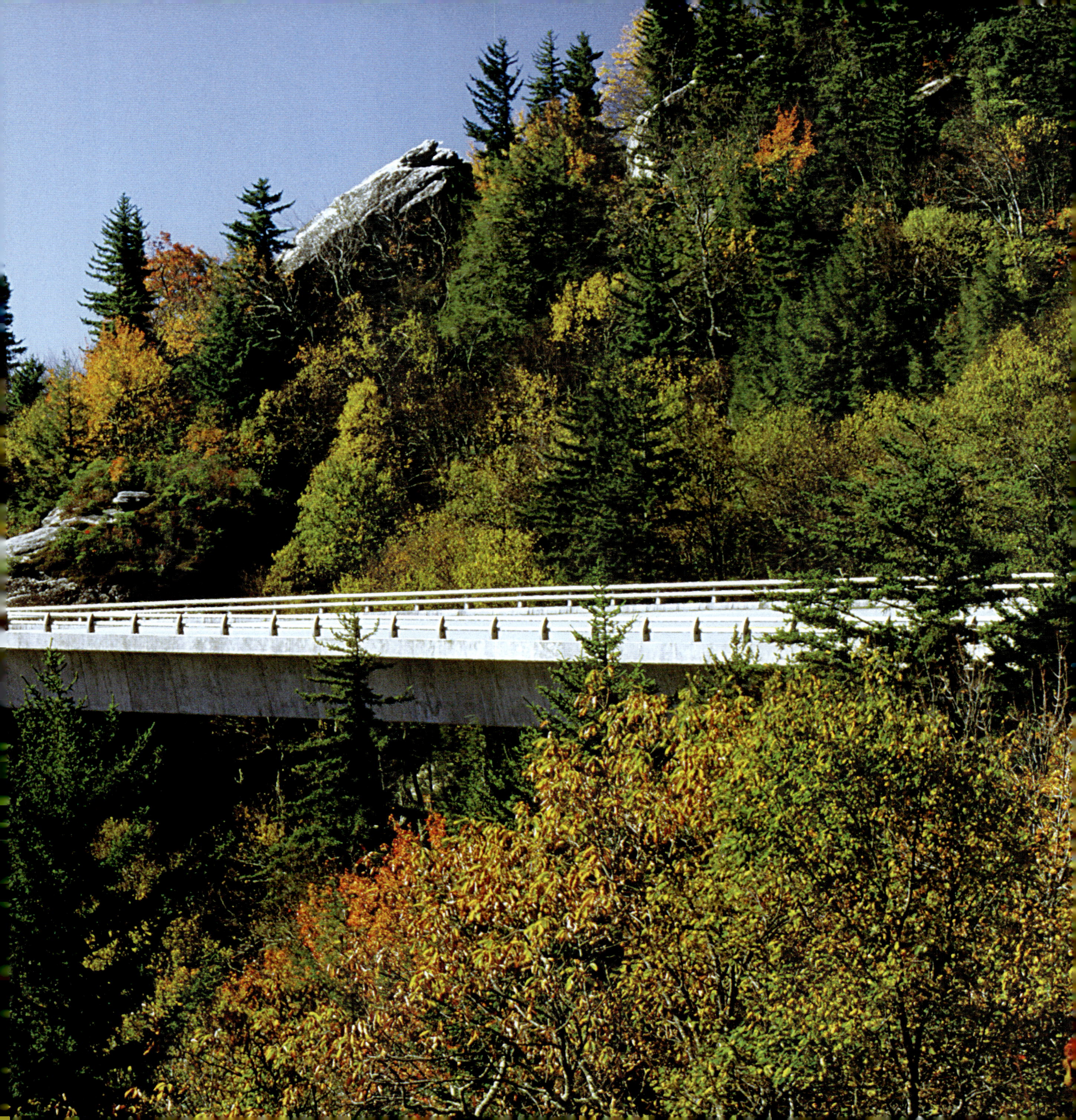

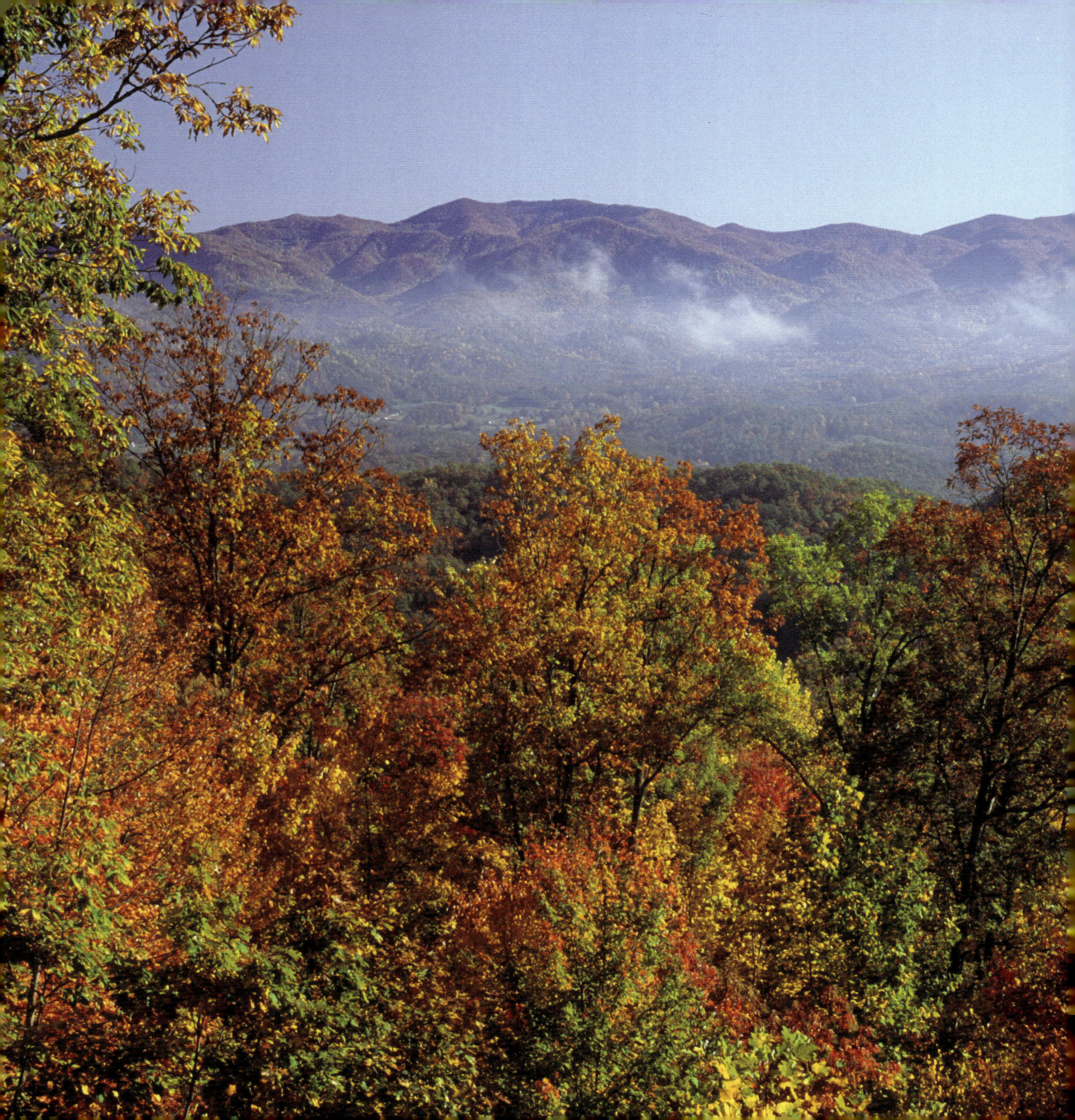

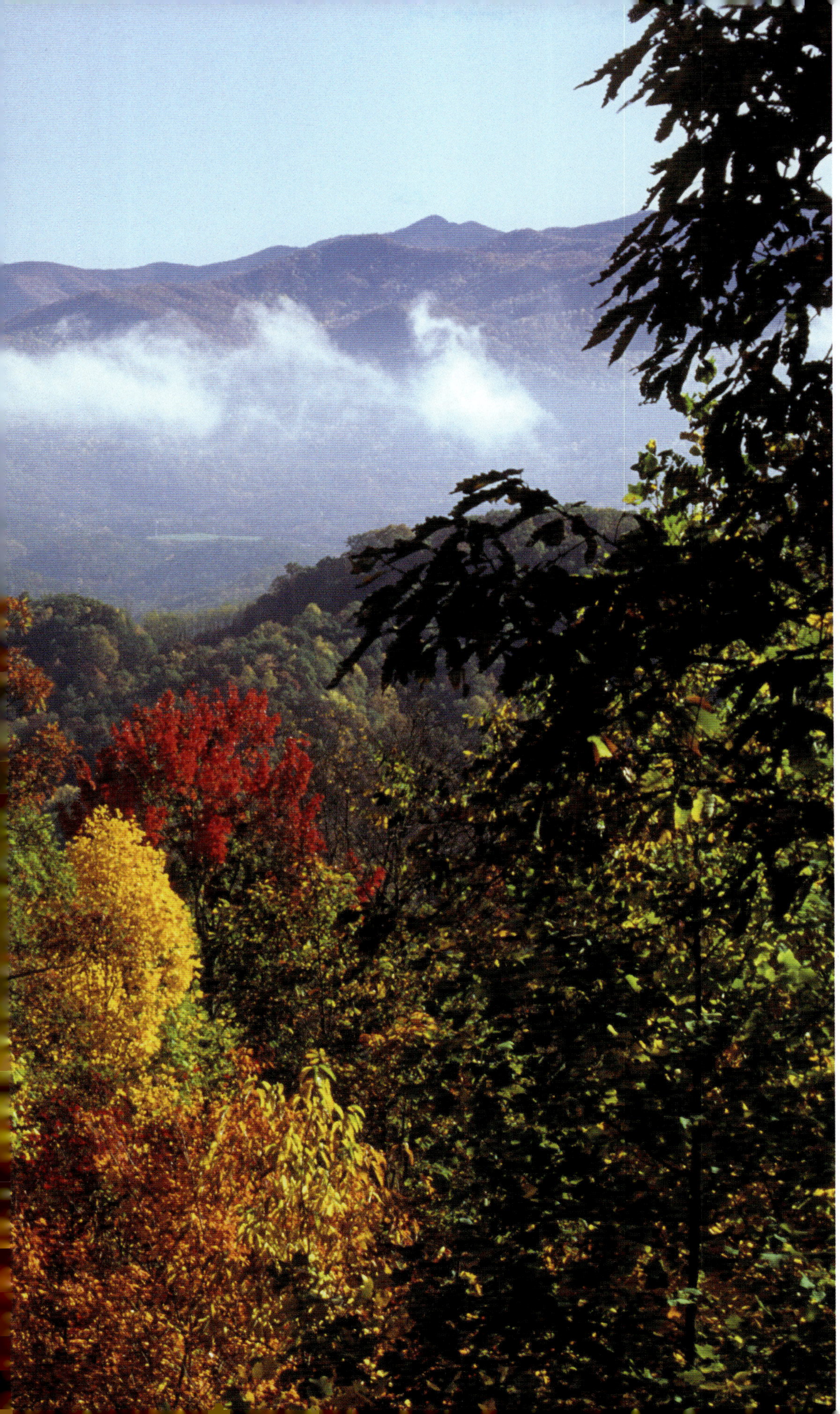

The aptly named Smoky Mountains can be seen rising above the clouds from this vantage point on Fry Mountain. These forested ridges straddle the border of North Carolina and Tennessee. Great Smoky Mountain National Park is the most visited in all of America, world renowned for its biodiversity and natural beauty.

PREVIOUS PAGE: Said to be the most complicated concrete bridge ever built, the Linn Cove Viaduct is 1,243 feet long, at an elevation of 4,100 feet. A key factor in the design was the minimal environmental impact to Grandfather Mountain, one of the world's oldest geological formations. It is a thrilling section of the Blue Ridge Parkway, ranked America's most scenic drive by leading travel writers.

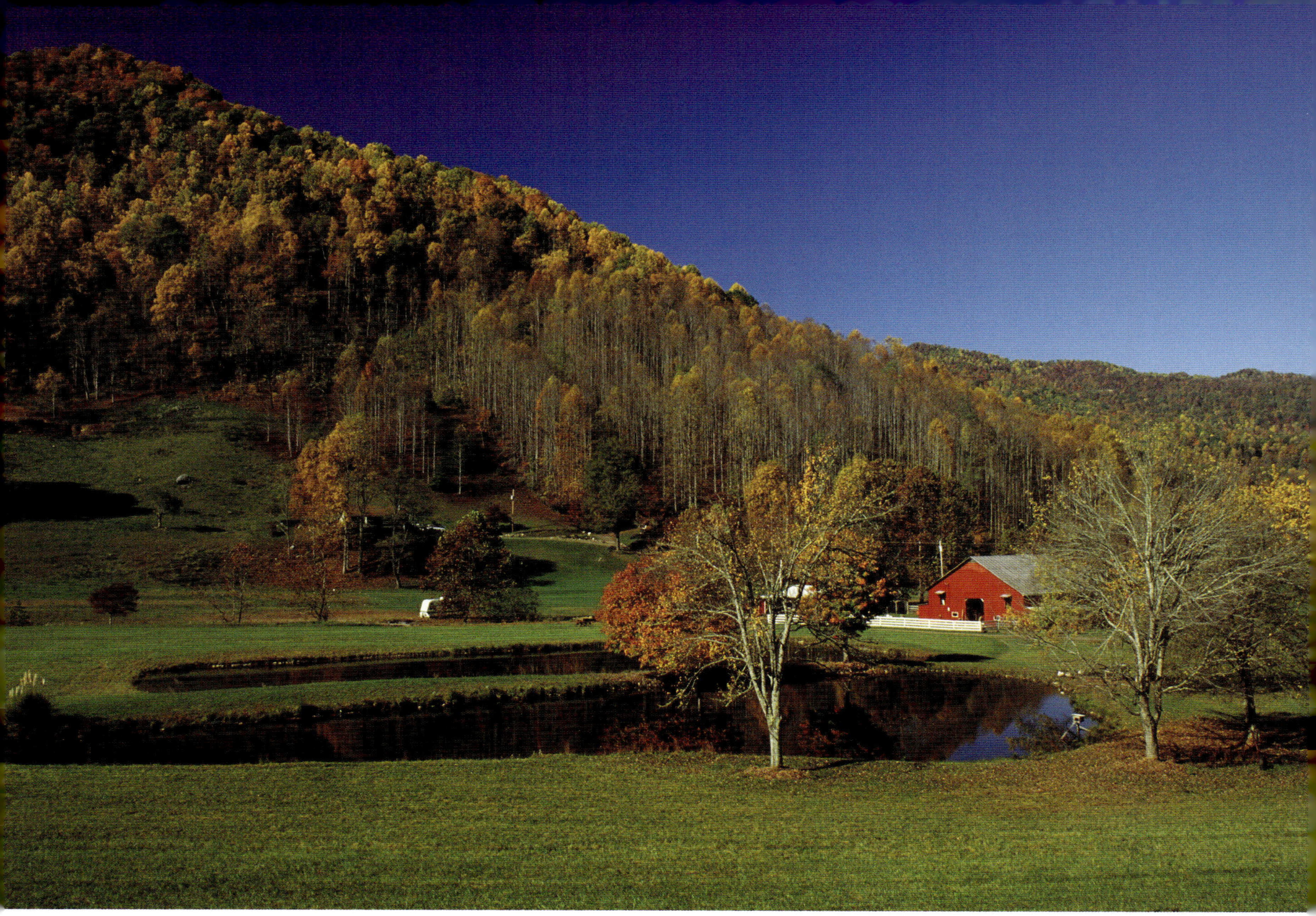

Tucked between the Great Smoky Mountains in western North Carolina, the long Tuckasegee River Valley in Swain County is part of the independently governed Cherokee Indian Reservation. Tuckasegee, or *daksi-yi*, means Turtle Place. Farming communities share this peaceful valley with bald eagles, herons and kingfishers.

OPPOSITE PAGE: The skiing is superb at Sugar Mountain, the largest ski area in North Carolina. Popular with families, it is one of the few eastern ski areas south of New England with a vertical drop over a thousand feet.

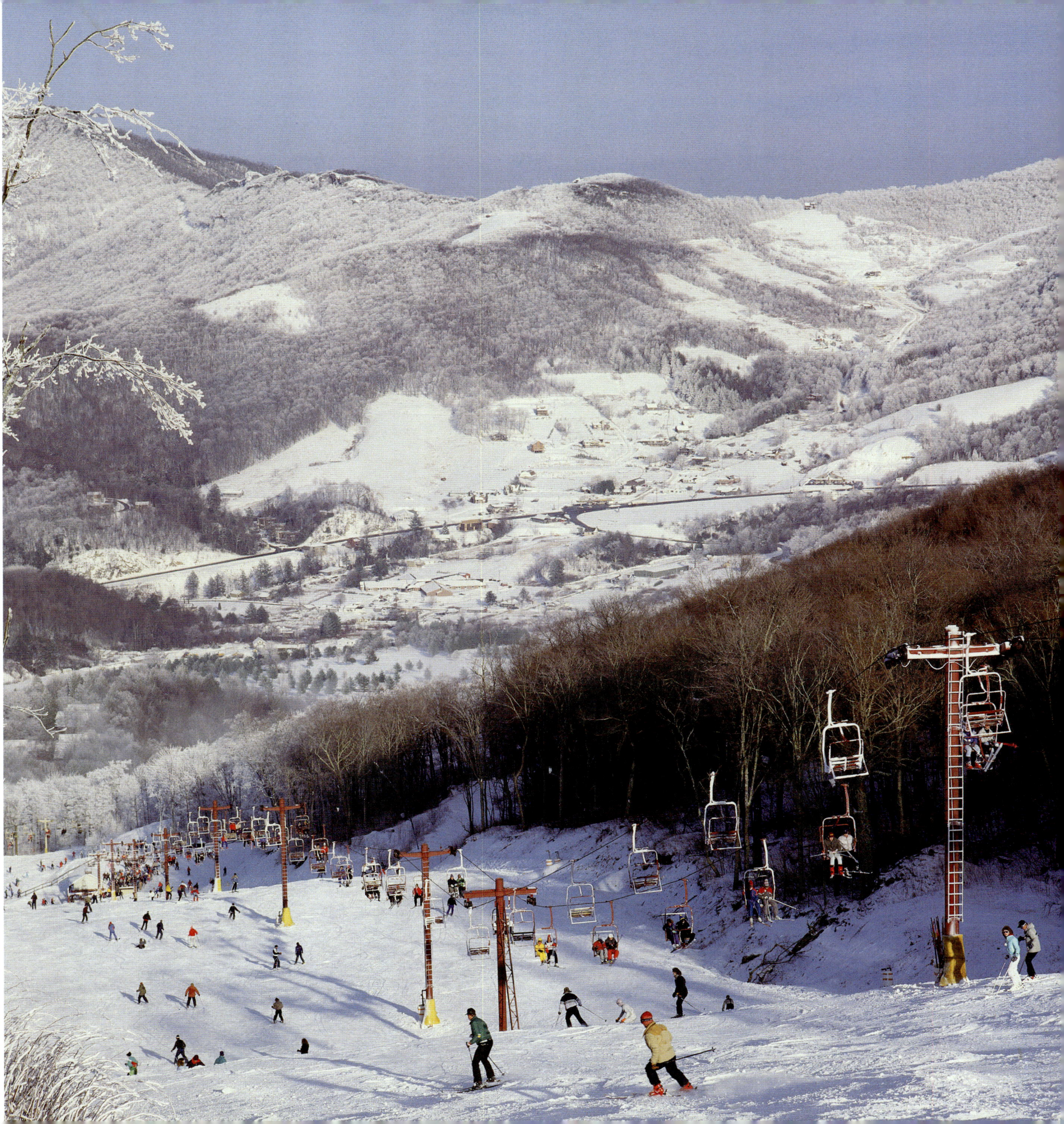

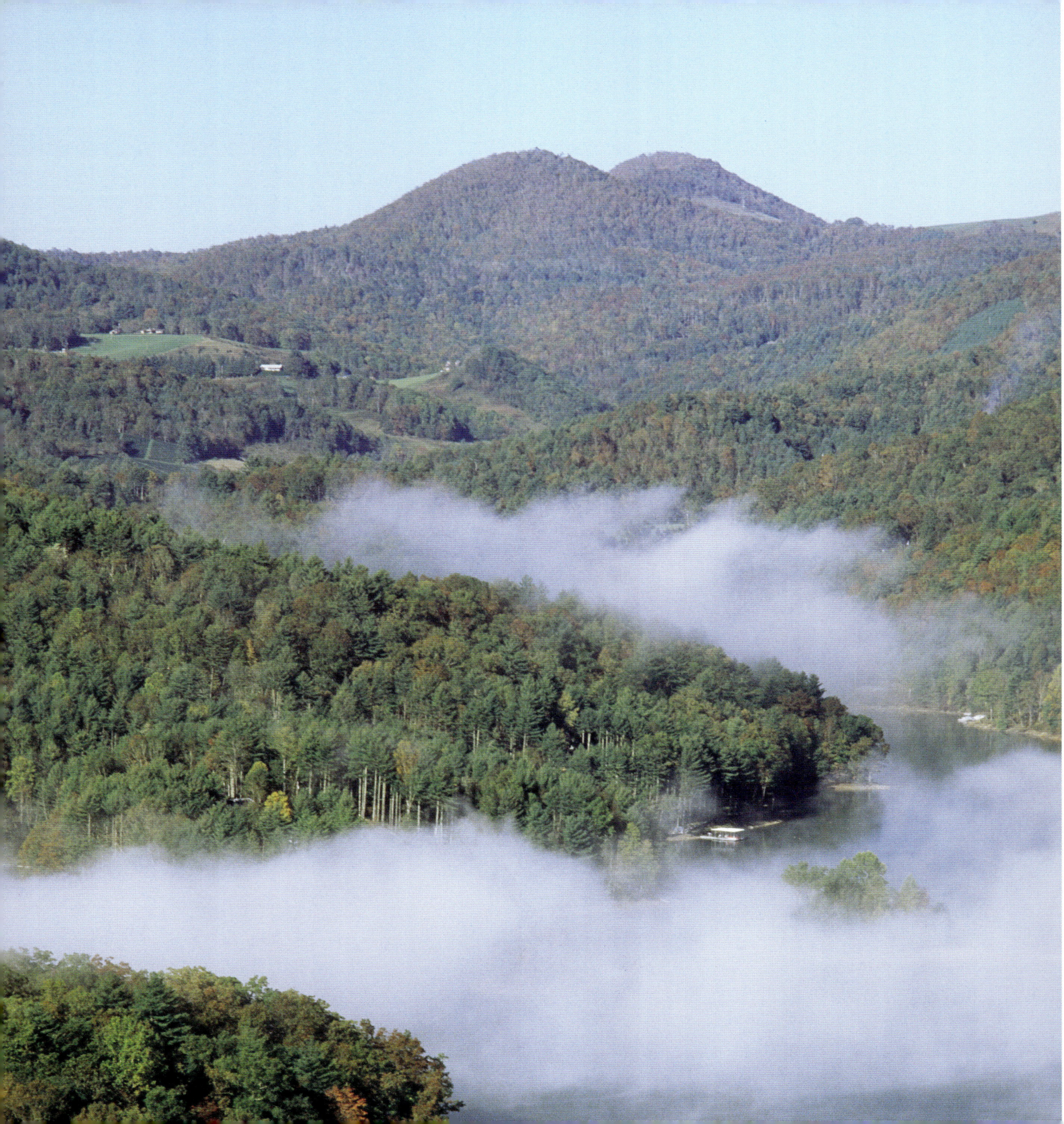

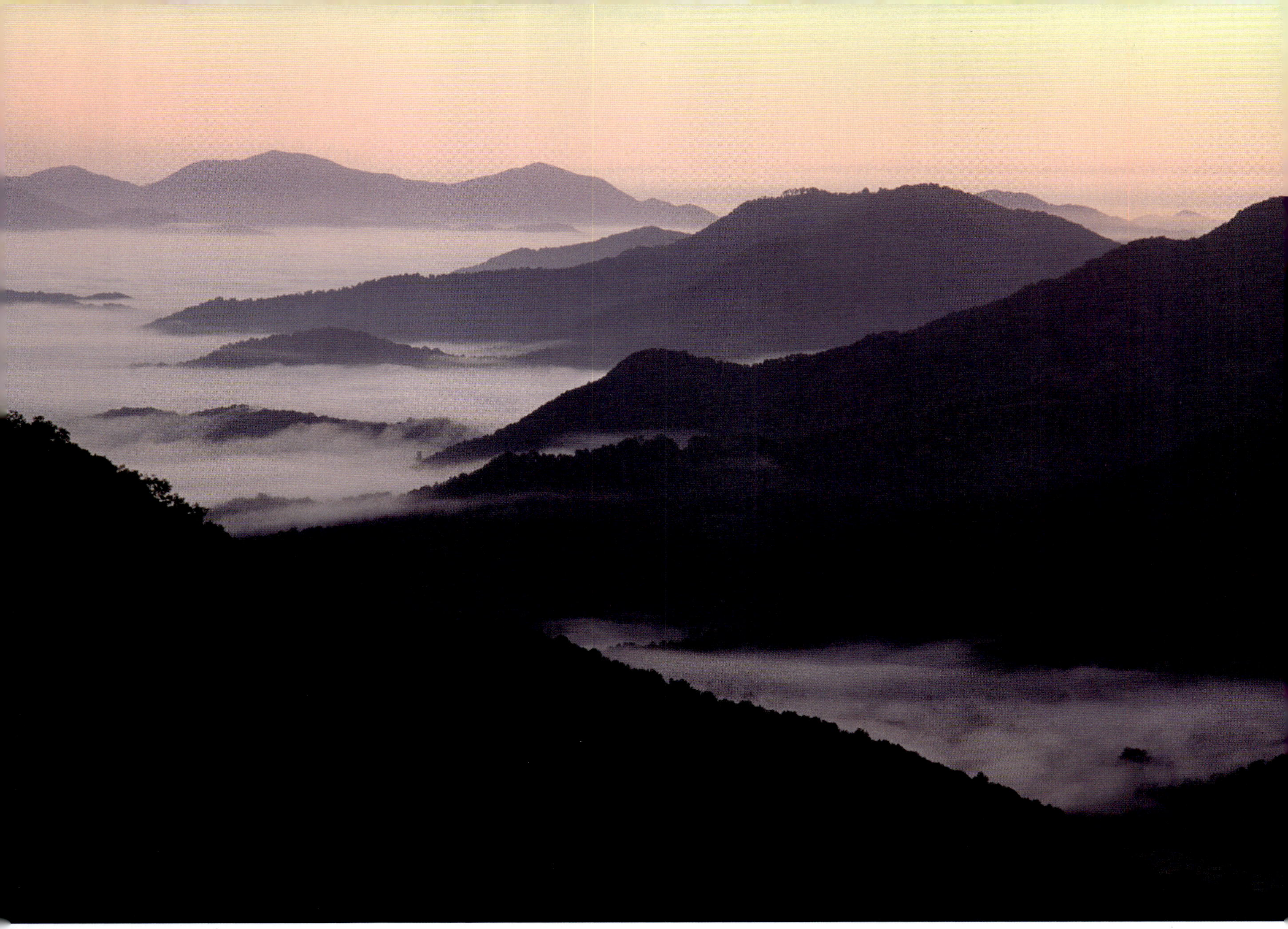

The sun rises over the majestic peaks of the Balsam Mountains in the Pisgah National Forest, as seen from the Waynesville Overlook. The Conservation Trust, funded by local residents, has protected stunning vistas such as this from development, maintaining the natural beauty of the landscapes.

OPPOSITE PAGE: The early morning mist tucks itself into the edges of Lake Glenville in the Upper Tuckasegee River Valley in the Balsam Mountains. The highest lake east of the Mississippi, it is considered one of America's 10 most beautiful lakes.

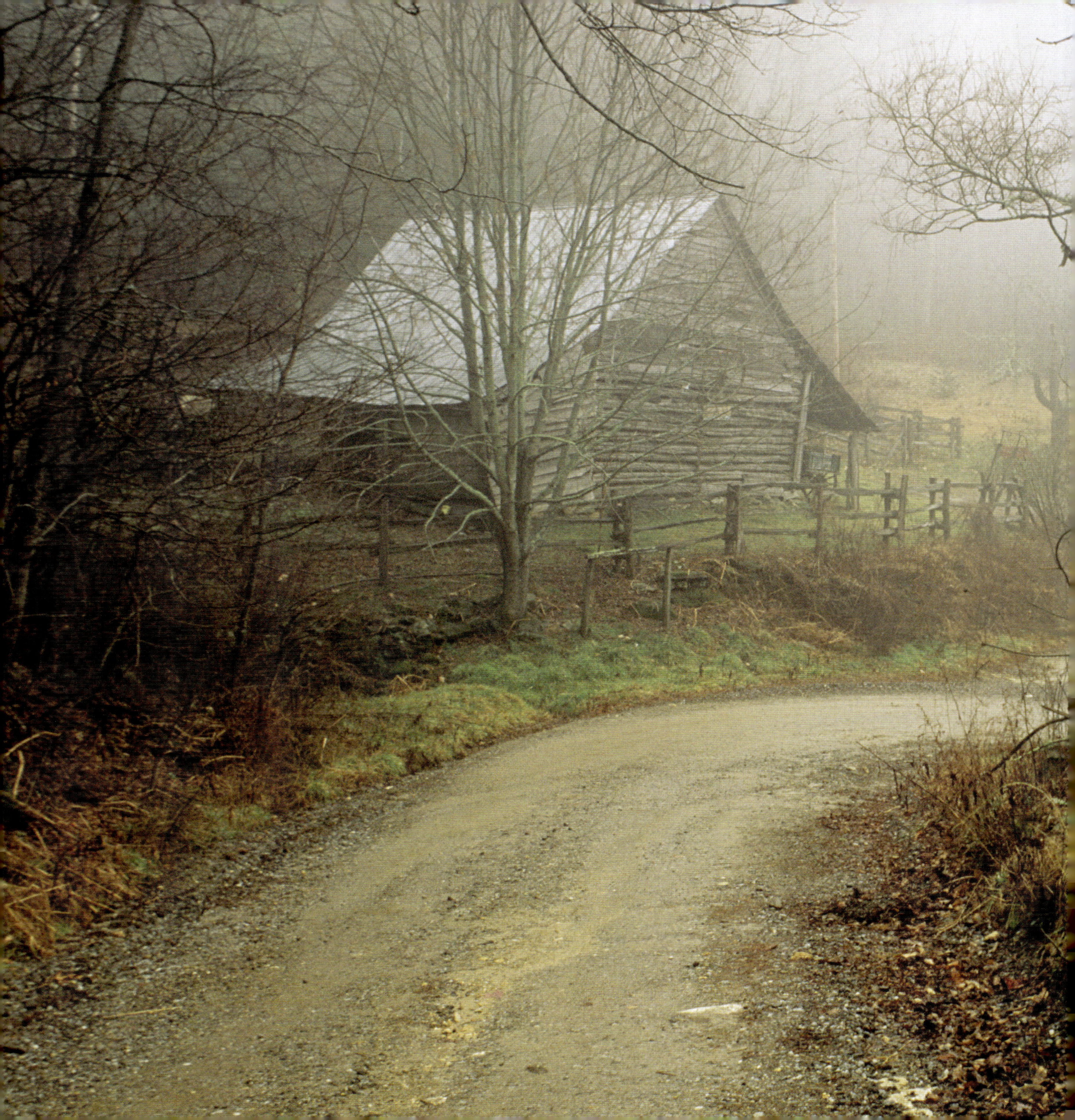

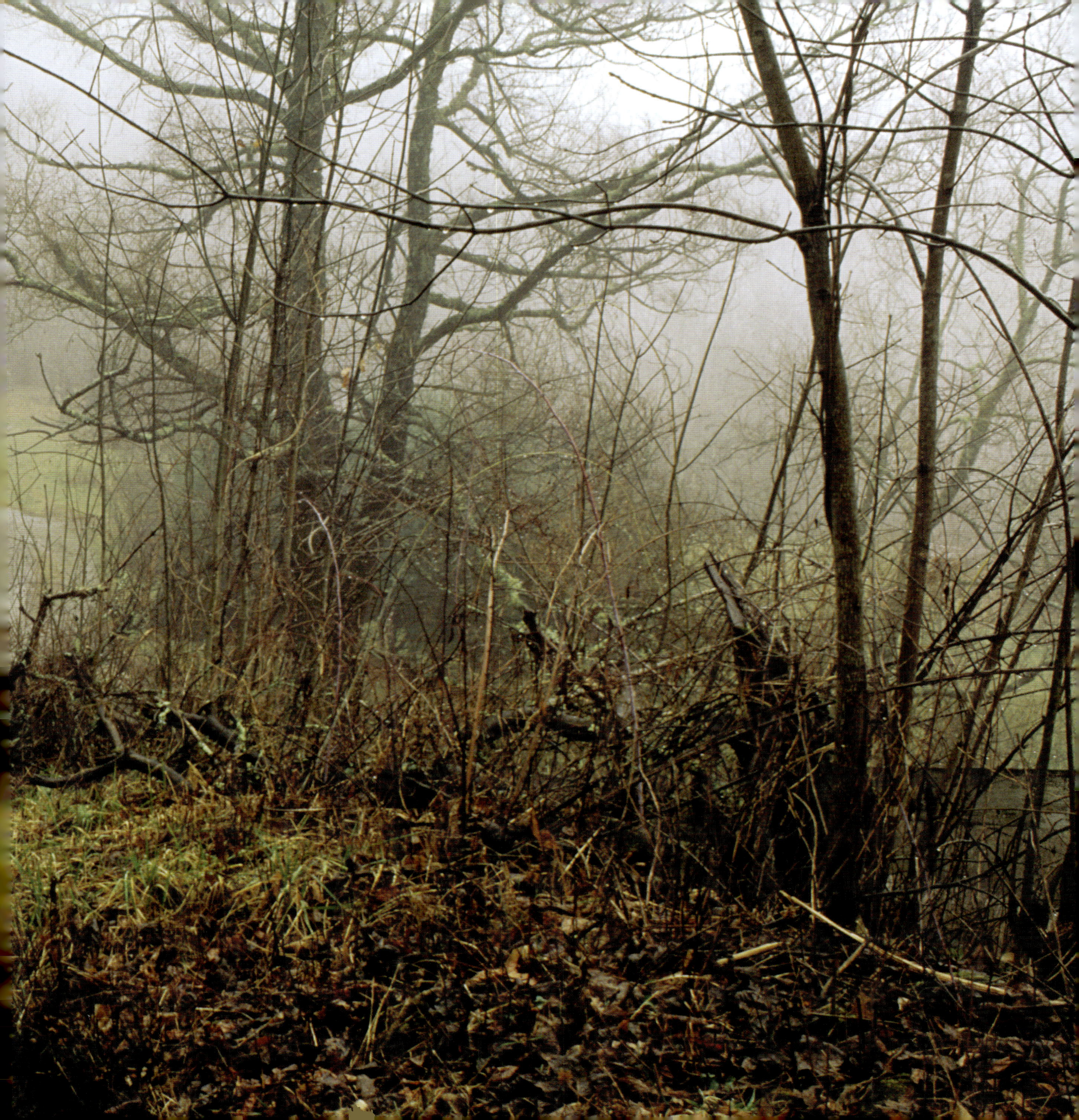

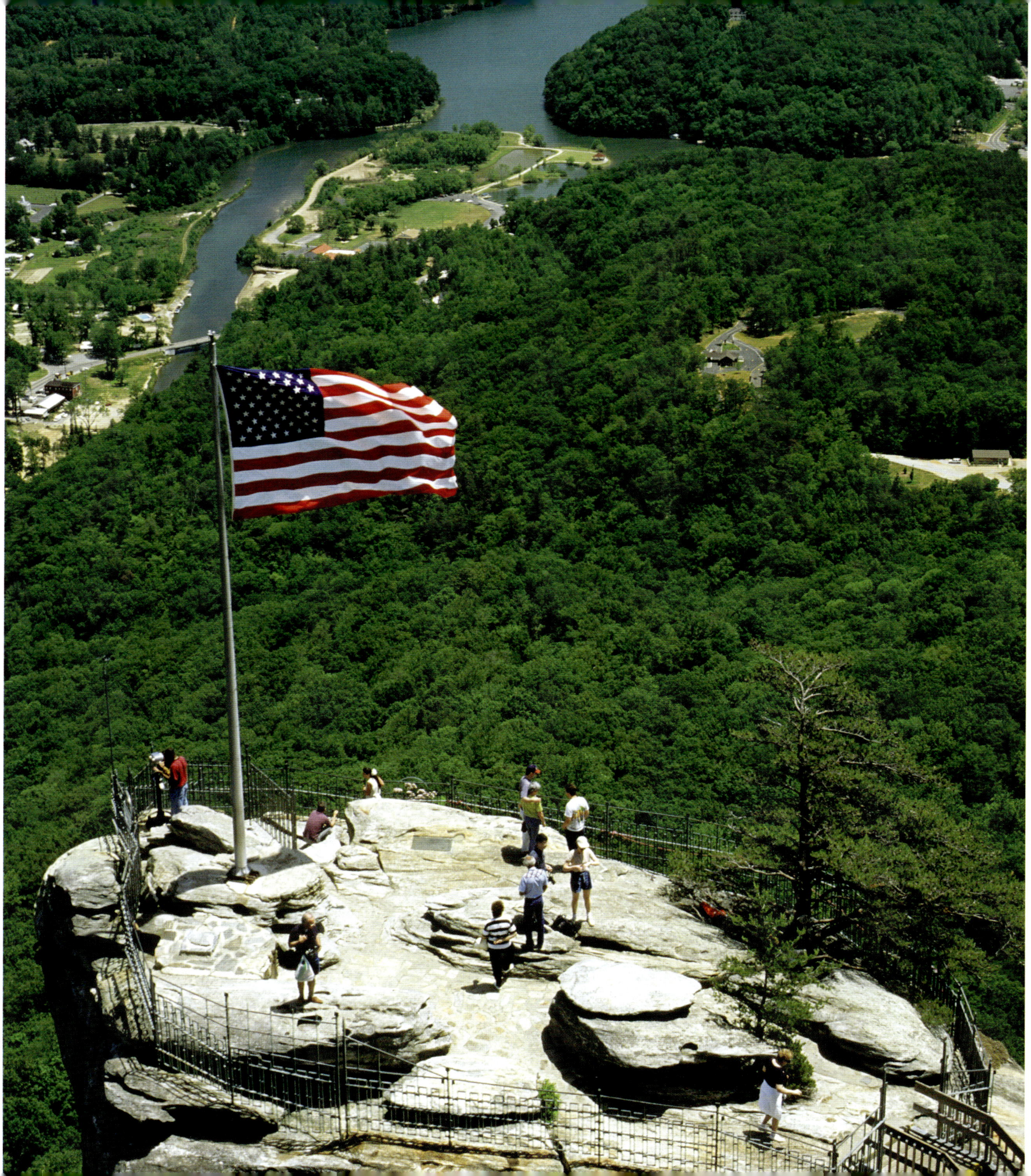

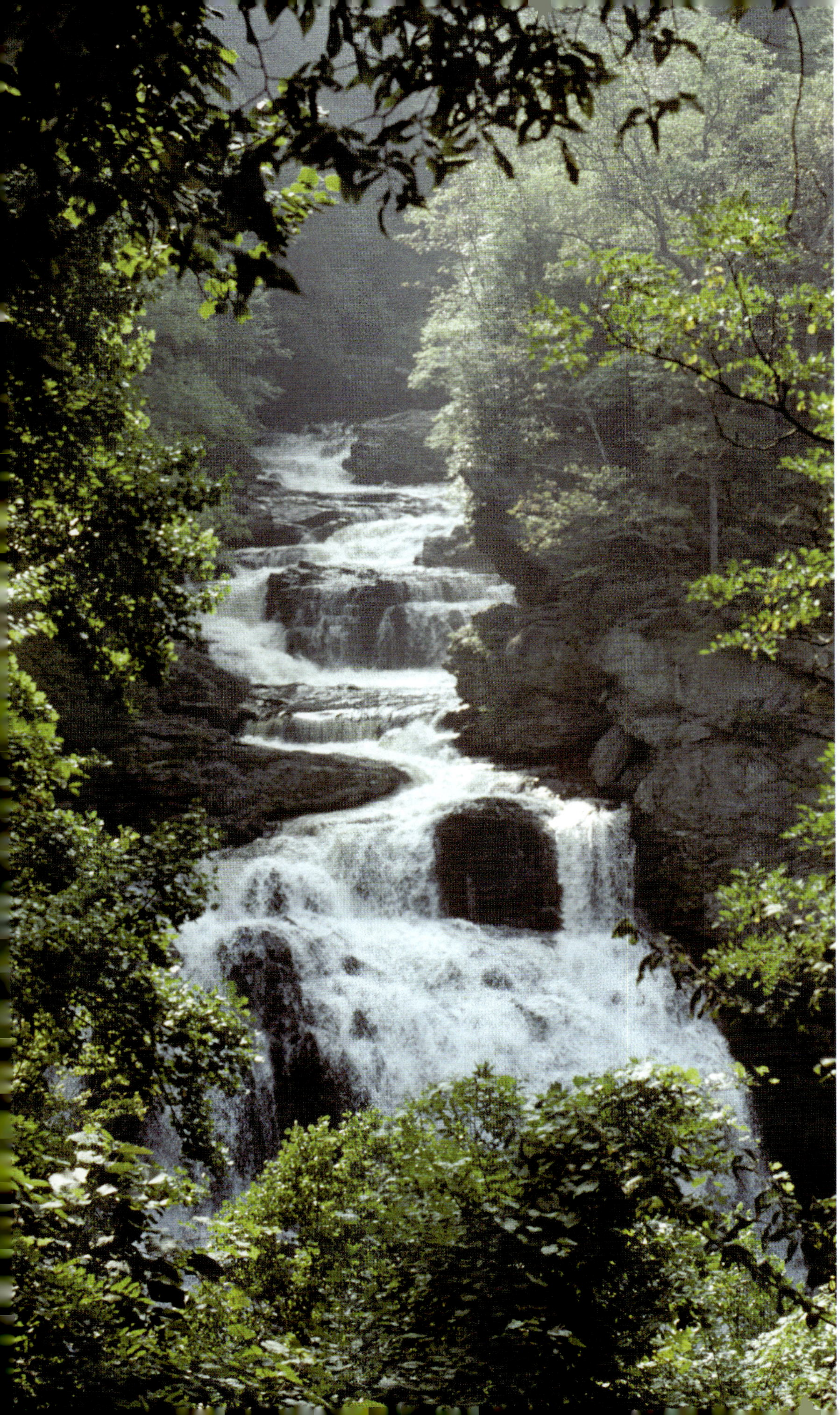

The Cullusaja Falls rush past the visitor from a height of more than 250 feet on the Mountain Water Scenic Byway. Situated in the spectacular Cullusaja River Gorge, this is one of North Carolina's most picturesque cascades.

OPPOSITE PAGE: Chimney Rock Park is a 1,000-acre scenic attraction with spectacular hiking trails, rock climbing opportunities and unique geological formations. Chimney Rock itself is a 315-foot granite monolith that offers 75-mile views. It towers above Hickory Nut Gorge, on the edge of the Blue Ridge Mountains.

PREVIOUS PAGE: Near Buck Gap and the highlands of the Smoky Mountains, in the northwestern part of the state, an old log barn hides in the fog. Part of the Blue Ridge National Heritage area, these mountains offer outdoor activities, cultural heritage, mountain crafts and theme parks.

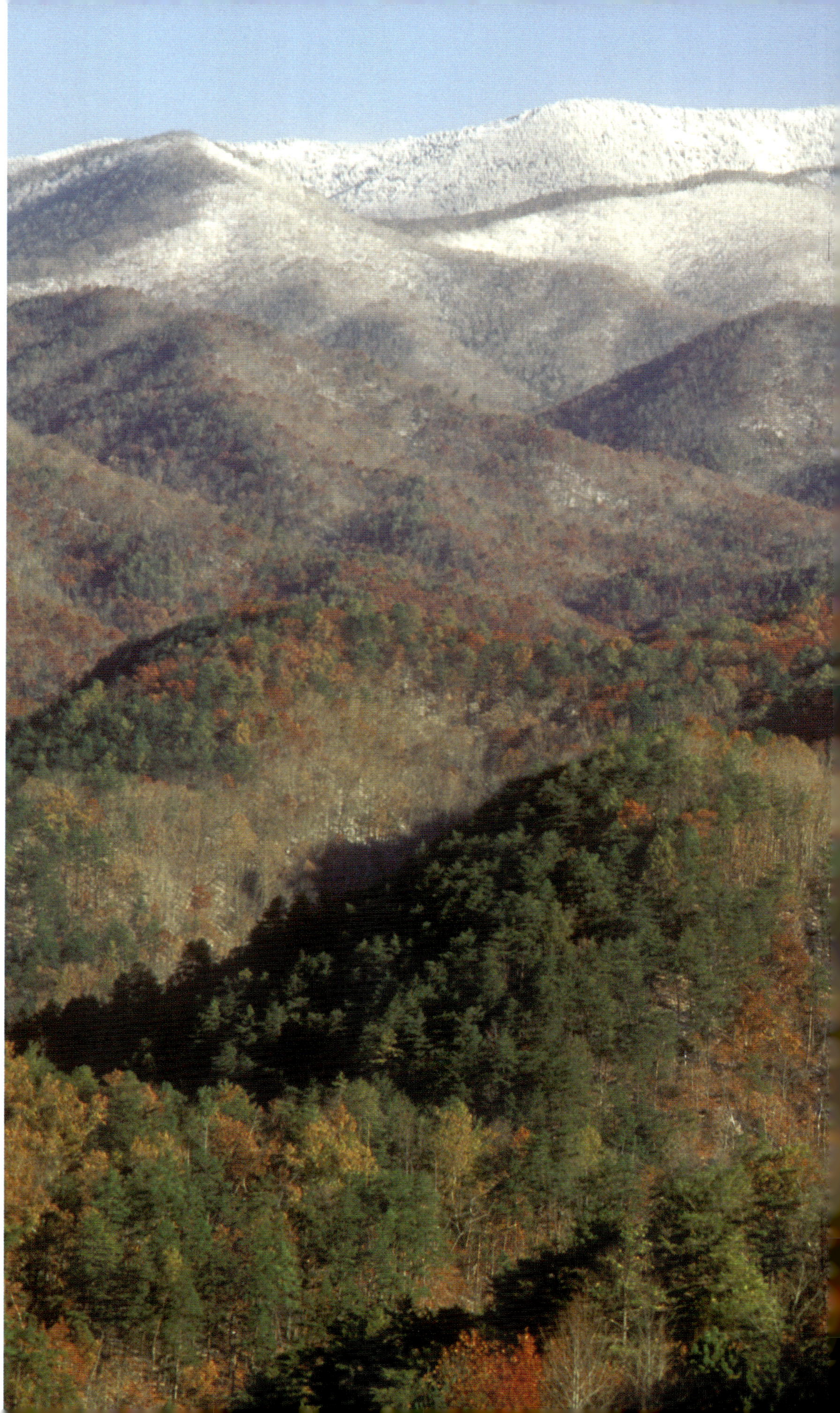

At an elevation of 6,643 feet, Clingman's Dome is the highest point on the Appalachian Trail and allows a 360 degree view of the Great Smoky Mountains. An observation tower sits on the state line between North Carolina and Tennessee.

FOLLOWING PAGE: The Appalachian Trail follows the beautiful 12-mile ridgeline called the Roan Highlands on a snowy winter day. But starting in mid-June, the same area is filled with the largest display of blooming rhododendron found anywhere in the world.

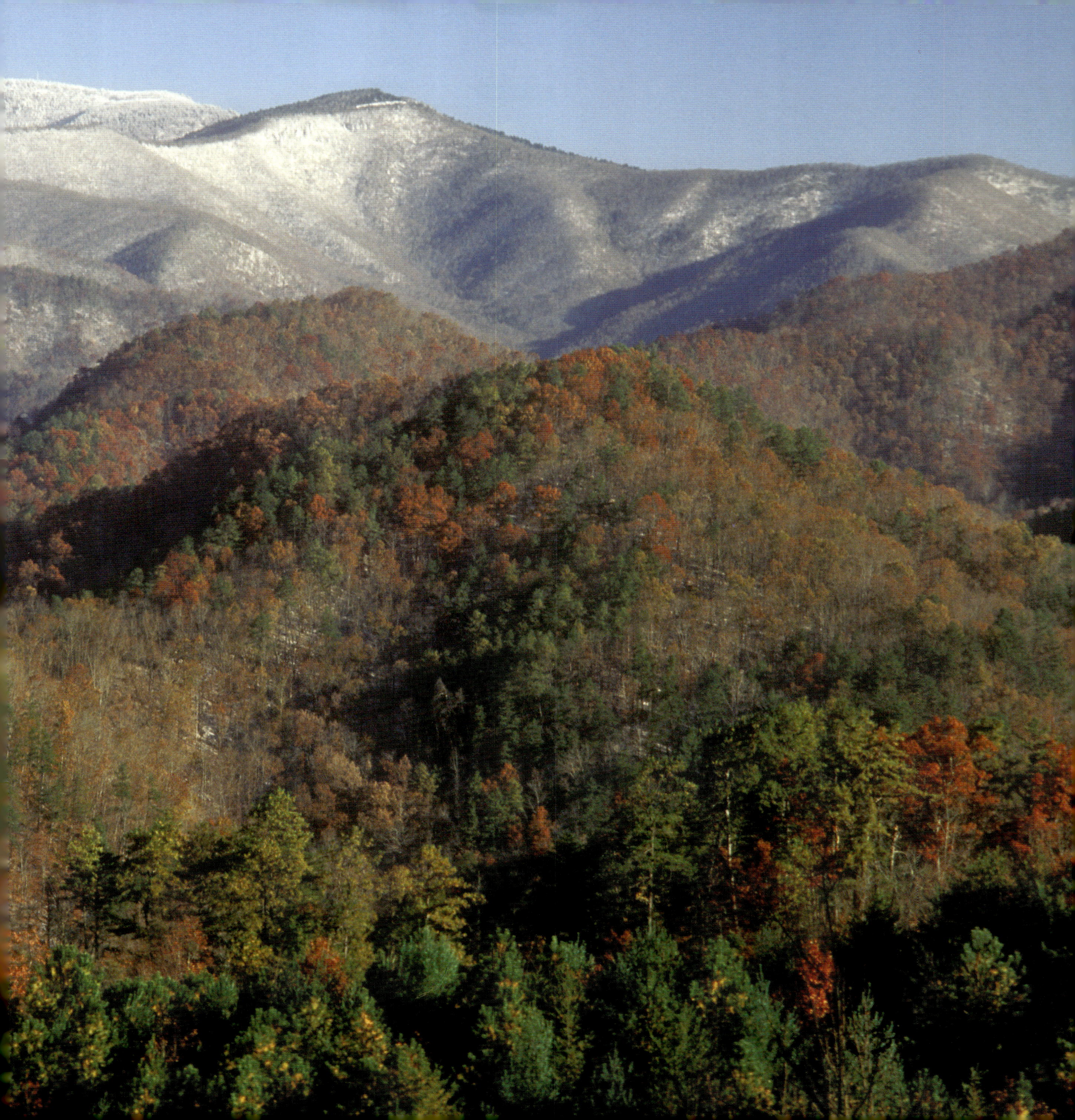

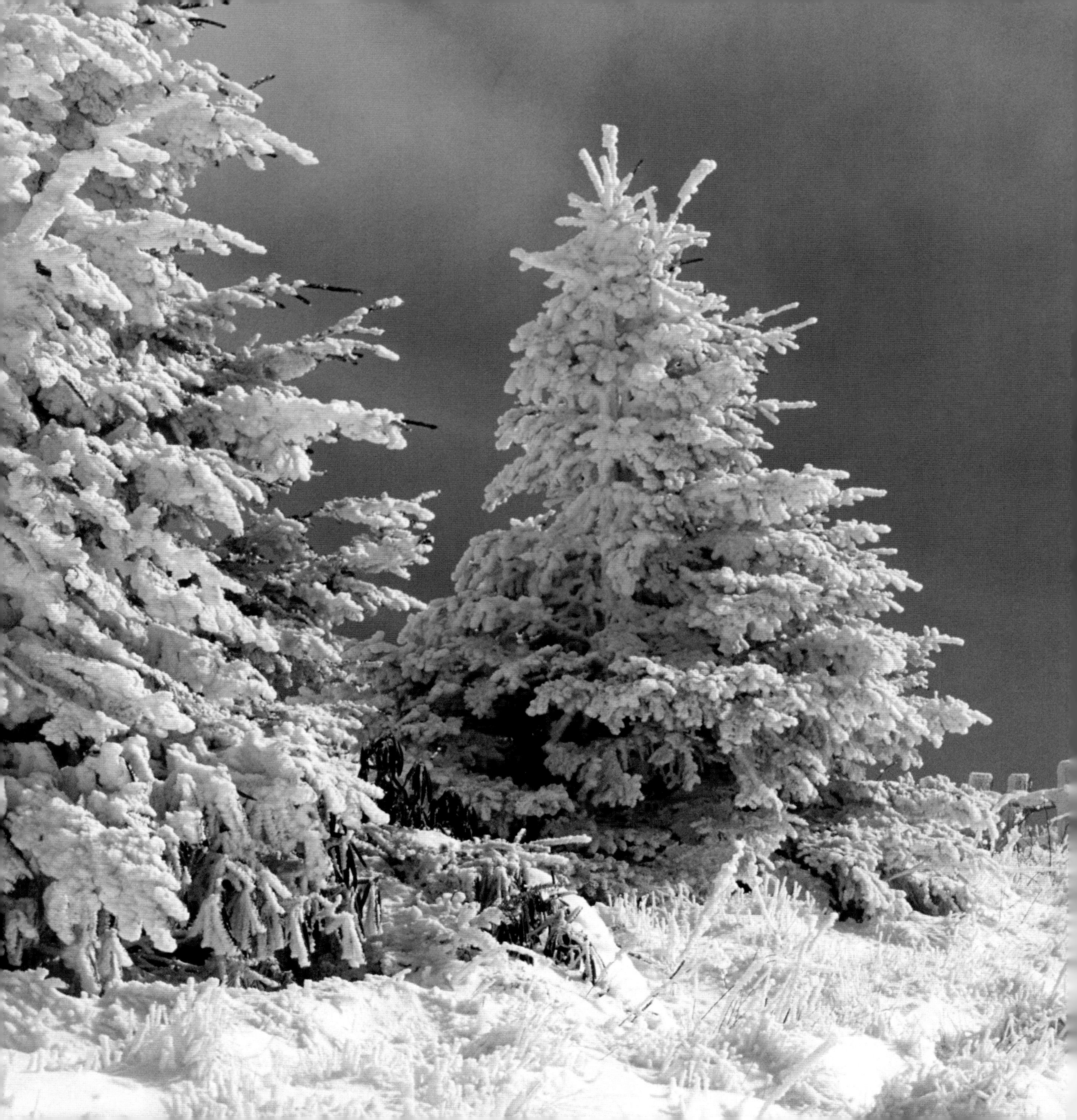

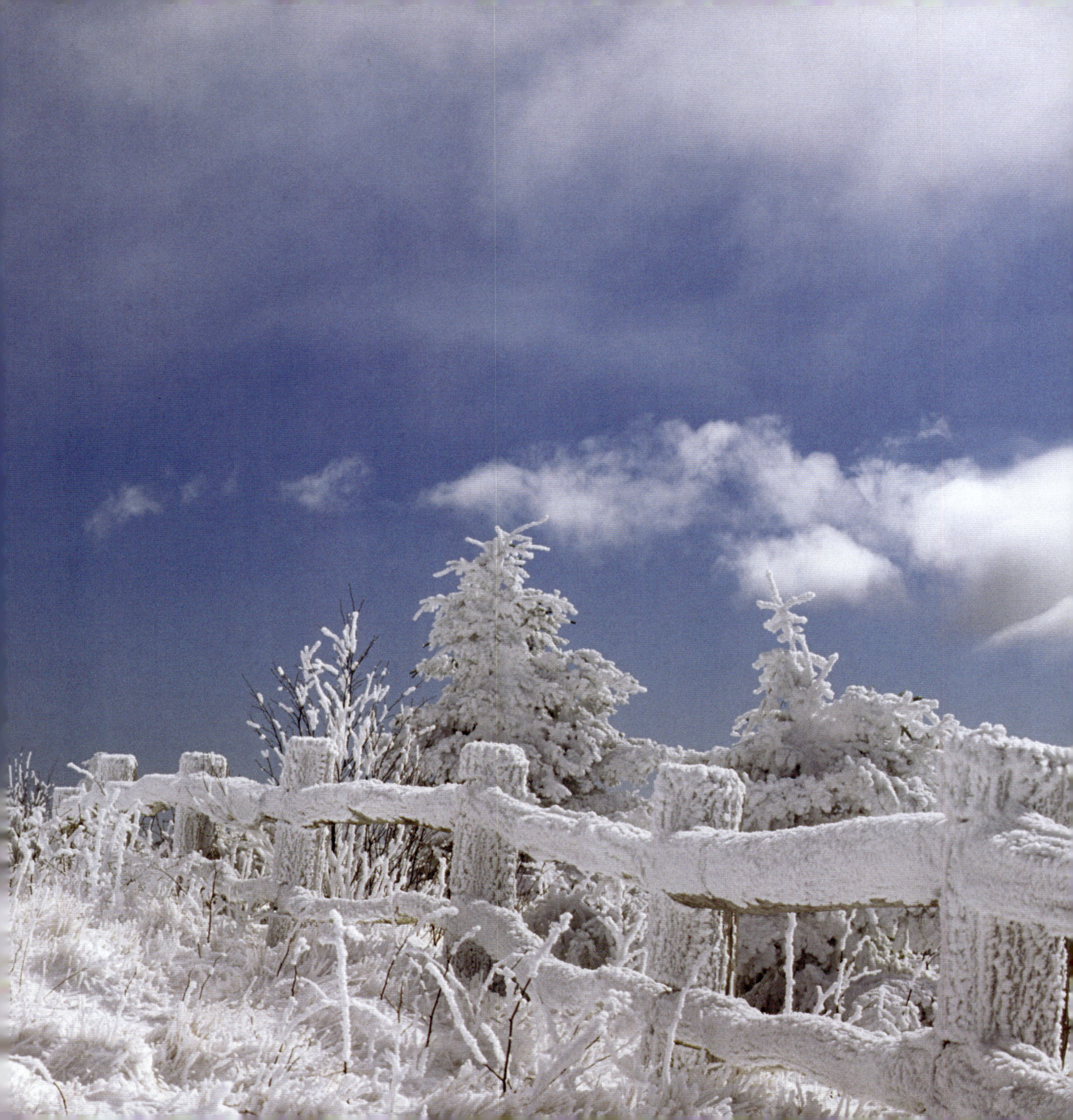

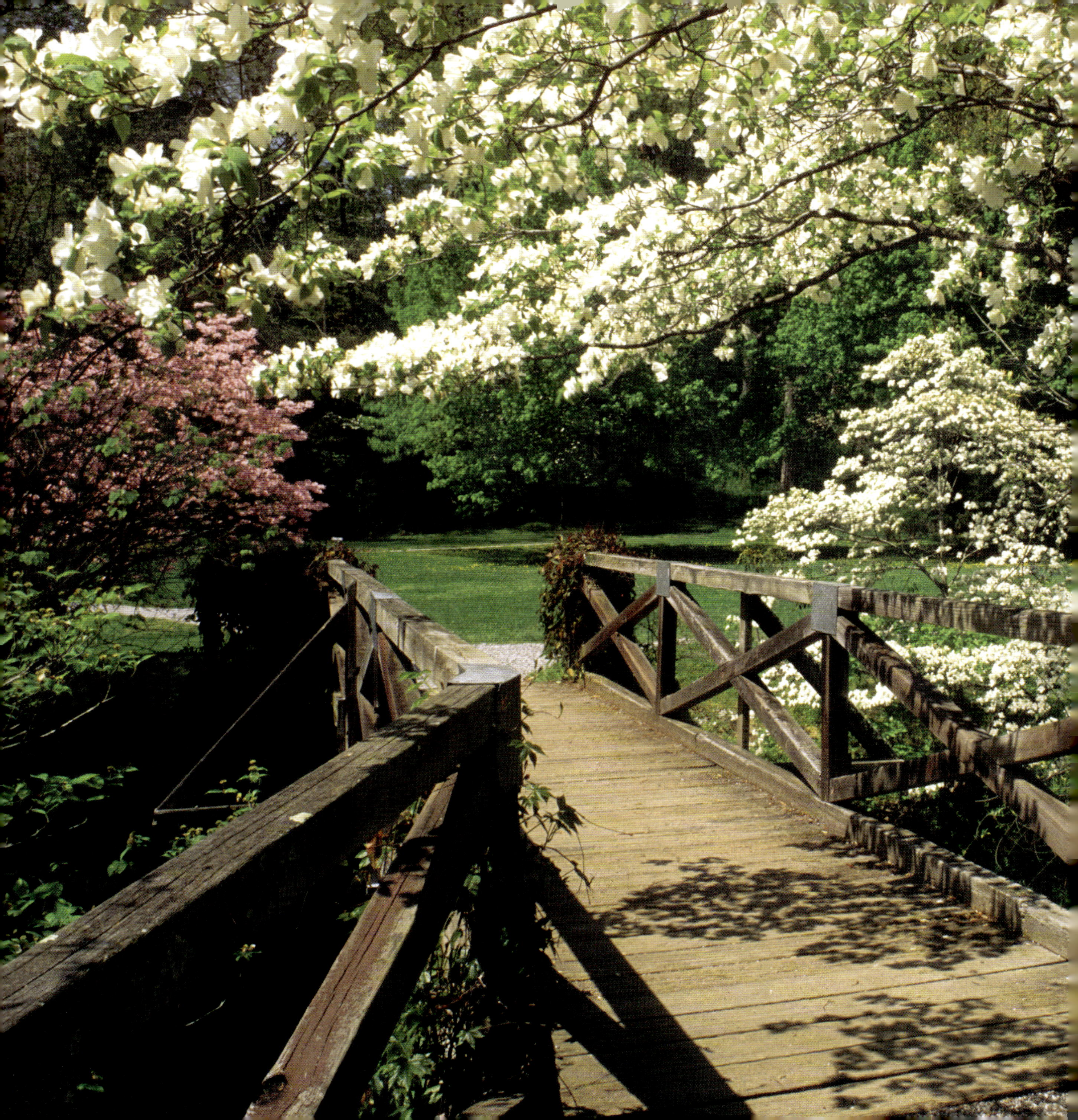

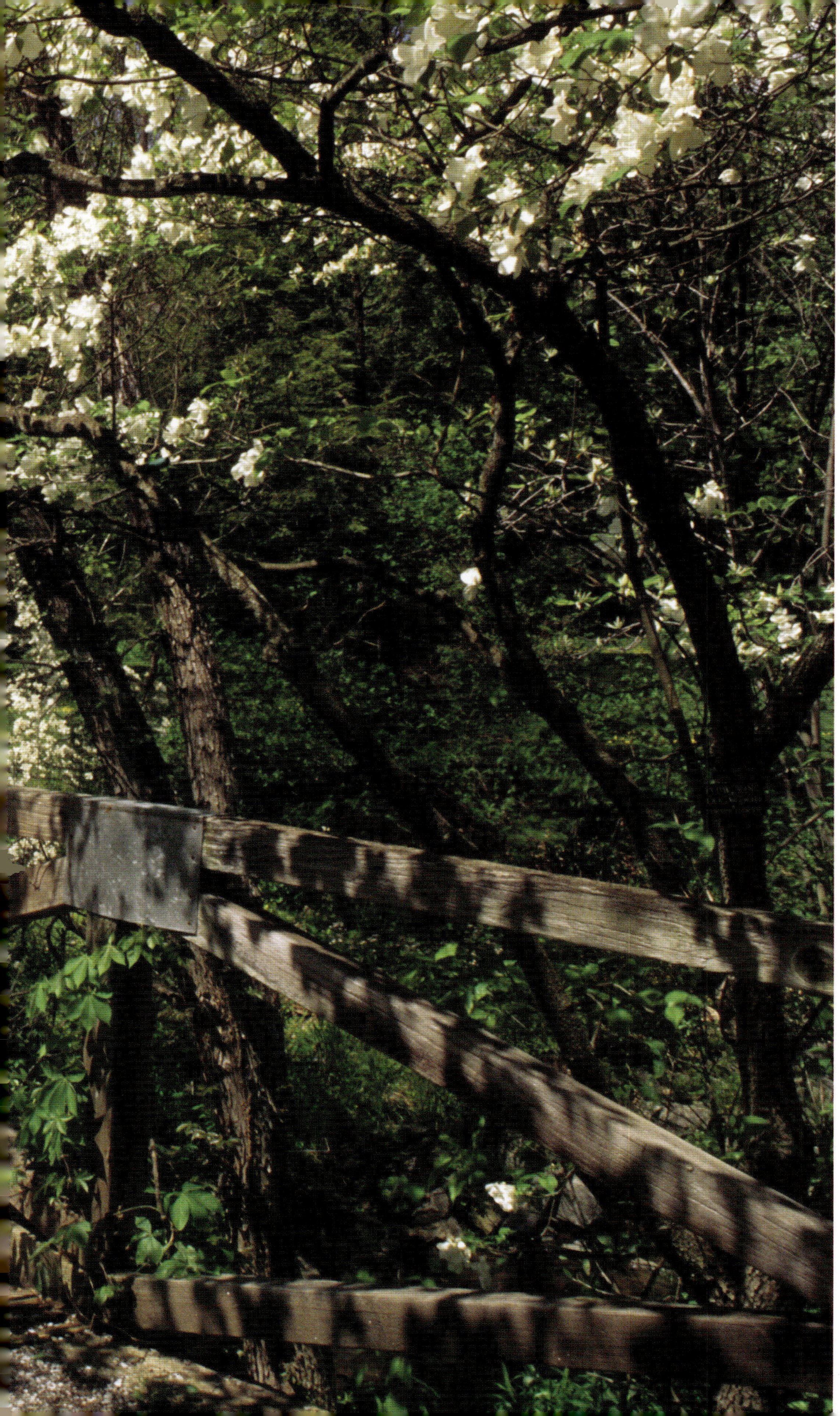

More than 600 species of plants native to the Southern Appalachians can be found in the 10-acre Botanical Gardens in Asheville, located in one of the world's most diverse temperate ecosystems. This footbridge is dappled by dogwood blossoms, the state flower.

FOLLOWING PAGE: Several picturesque small towns are nestled into the forested slopes of the Blue Ridge Mountains. Waynesville offers a great variety of attractions, including folk art, historical exhibits and easy access to wonderful outdoor activities such as river rafting, hiking and horseback riding.

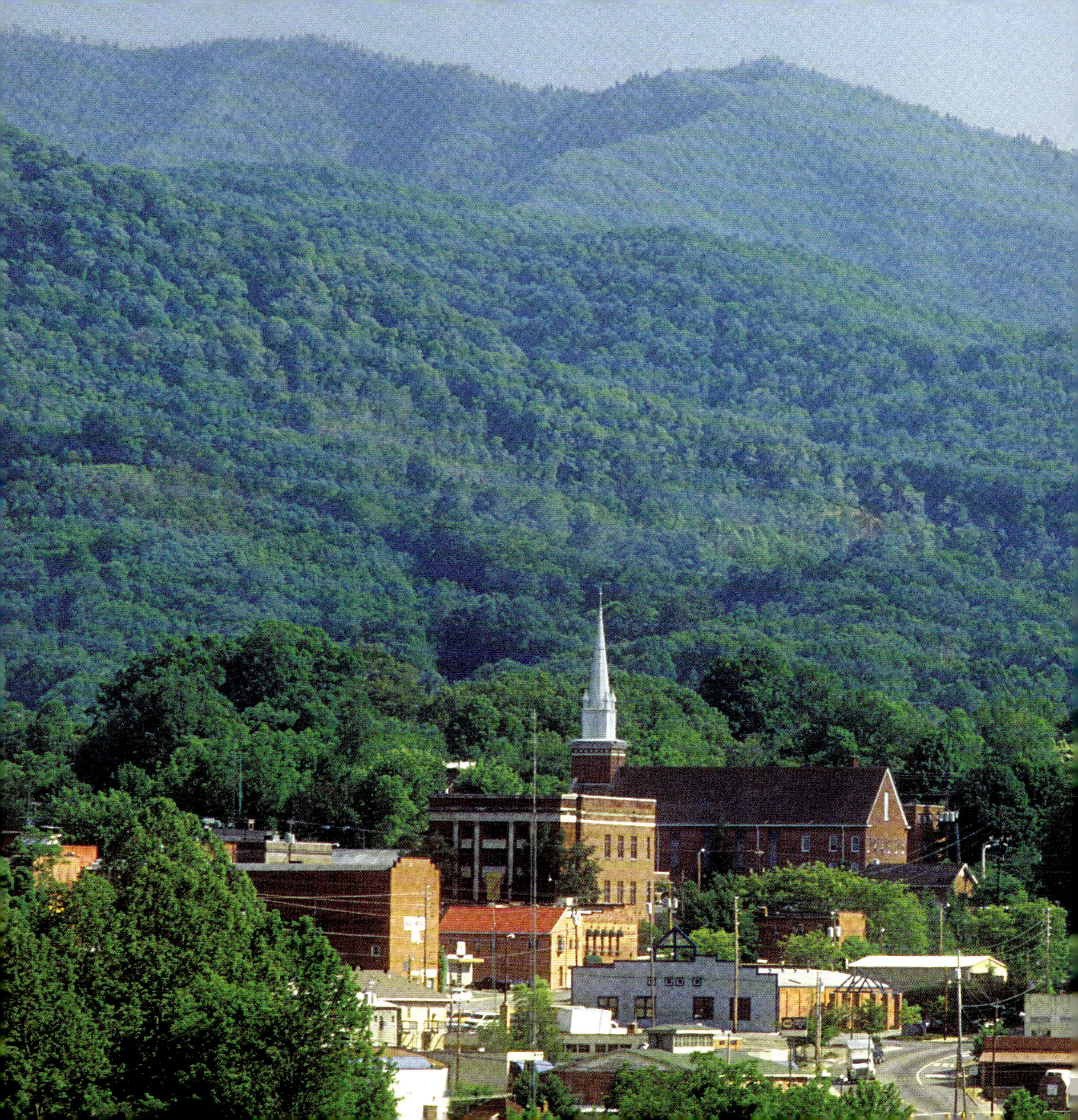

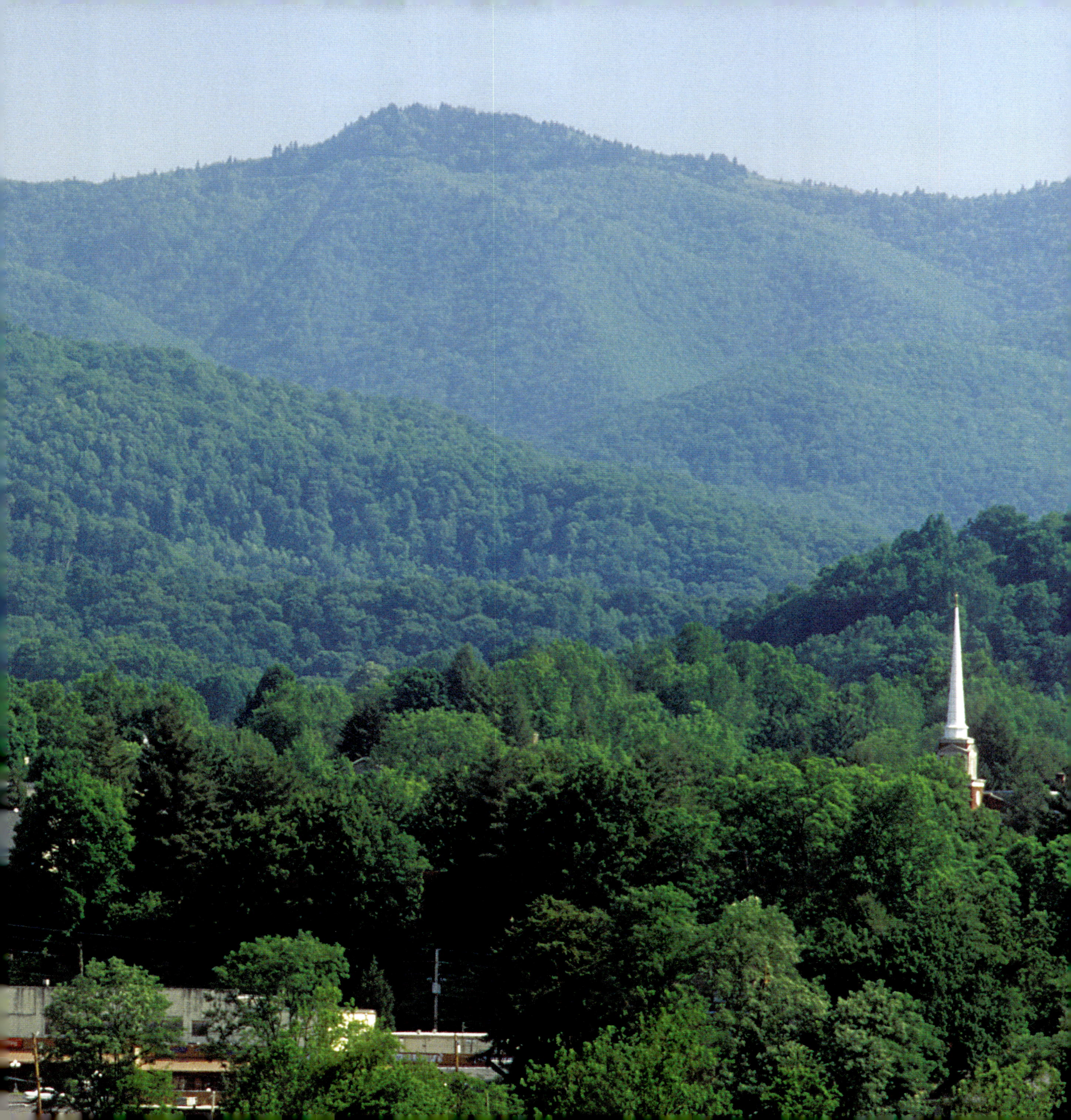

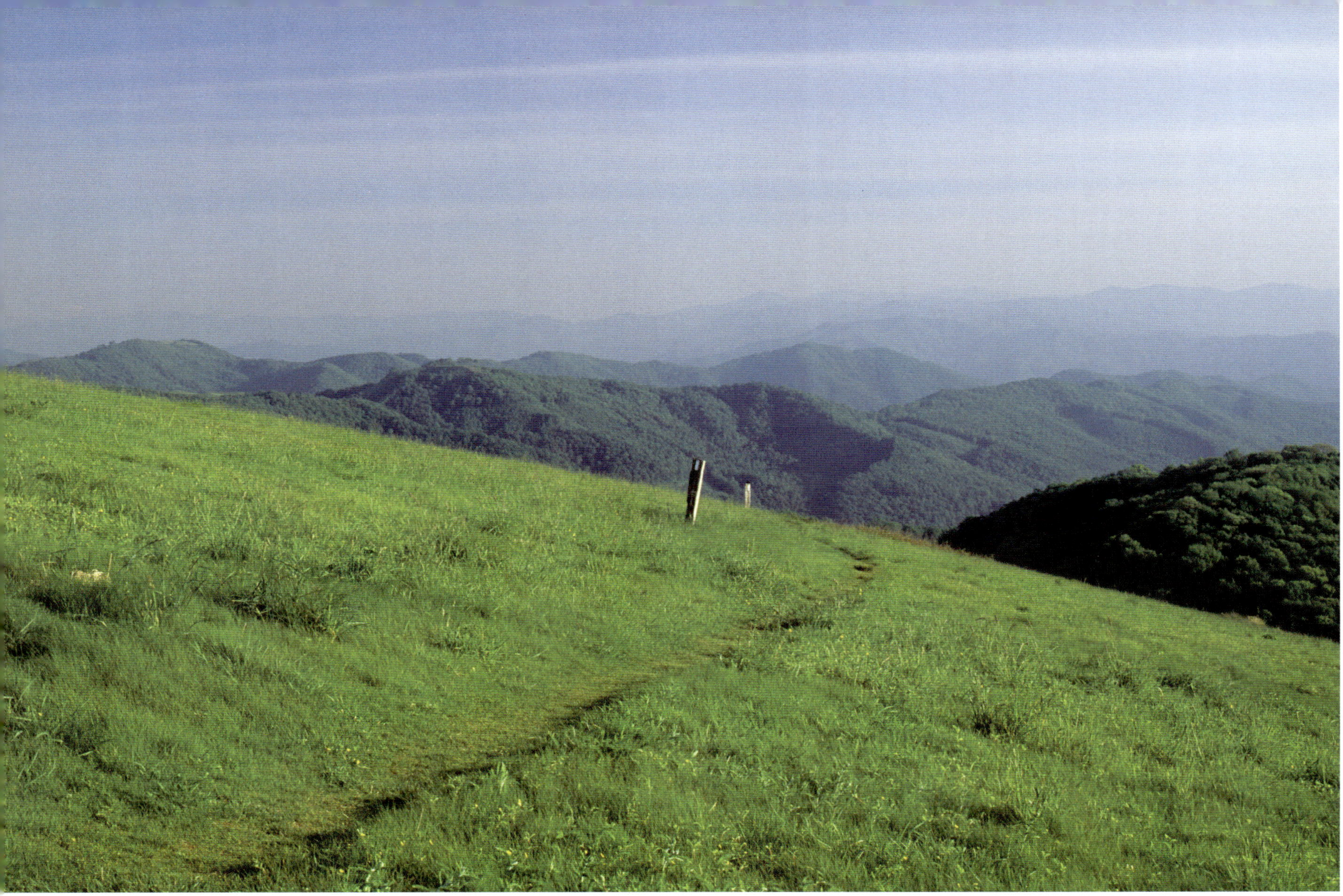

Max Patch is one of the many lush meadows on the summit of the Appalachian Trail. It is located near the town of Hot Springs, a favored destination since the early 1800s, famous for its healing mineral waters and magnificent mountain views.

OPPOSITE PAGE: Yancey County sits surrounded by the Blue Ridge Mountains. Visitors discover delightfully quaint place names such as Bee Log, Pig Pen and Hardscrabble. Here, fields of tobacco are drying in the afternoon sun in the community of Possum Trot.

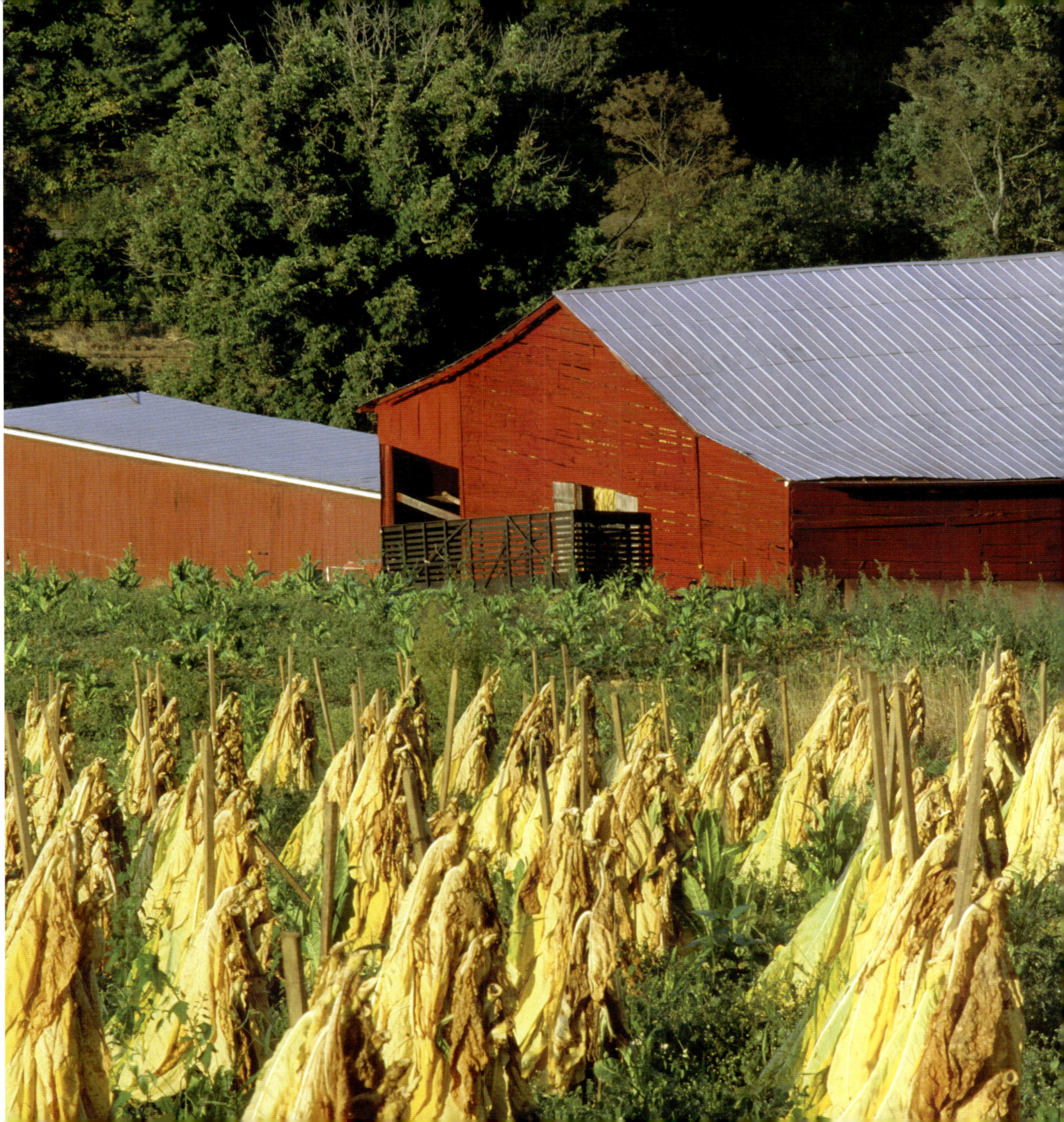

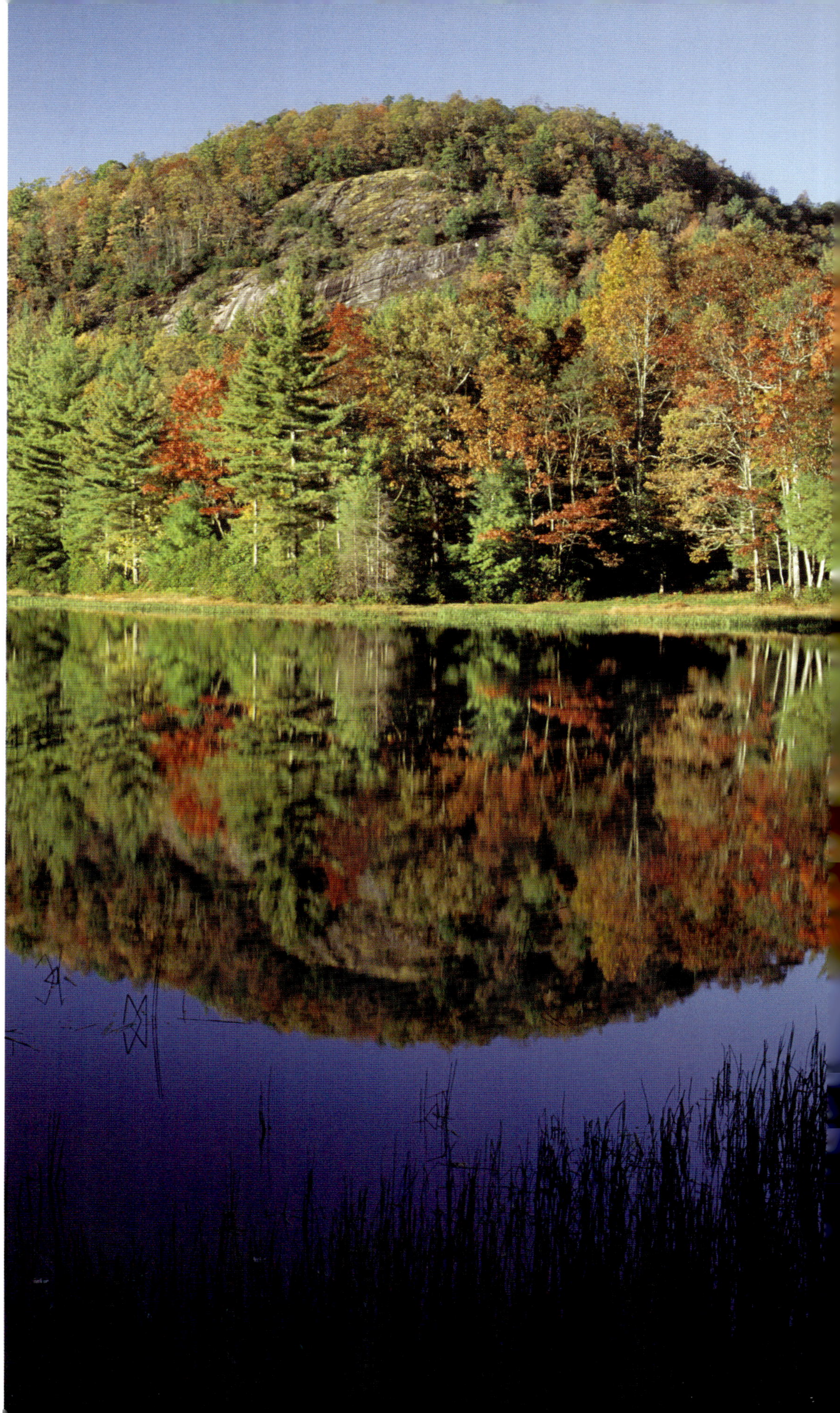

Double Knob is a mountain summit in Jackson County in the southwest arm of the state. At 4,432 feet above sea level, it reflects its autumn glory in a small lake. Mountain biking, hiking and climbing trails challenge and inspire the visitor.

OPPOSITE PAGE: This pioneer homestead is the birthplace of Governor Zebulon Baird Vance, a Civil War officer and U.S. senator. It has been reconstructed around the original chimneys in the period style of 1790–1840.

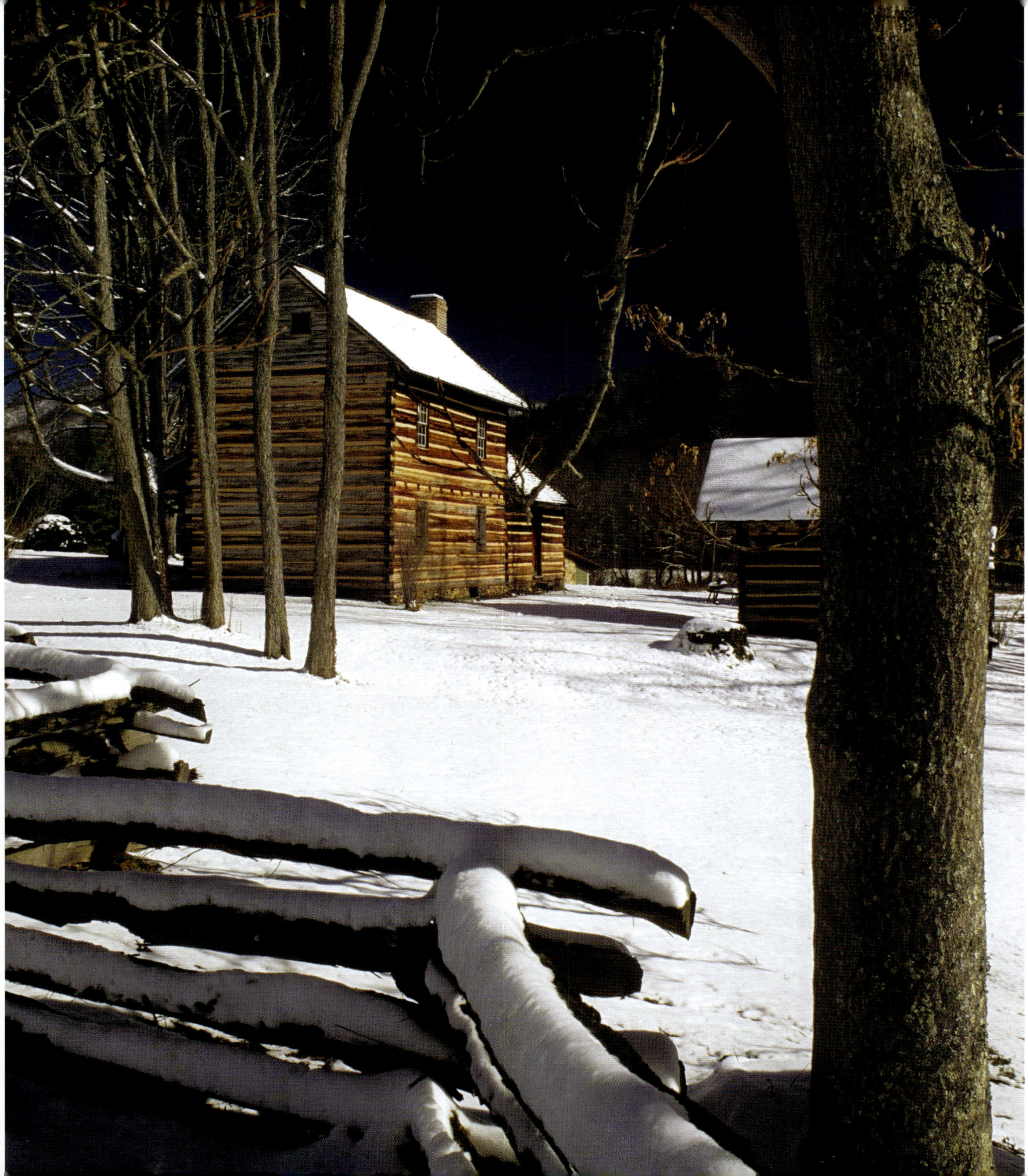

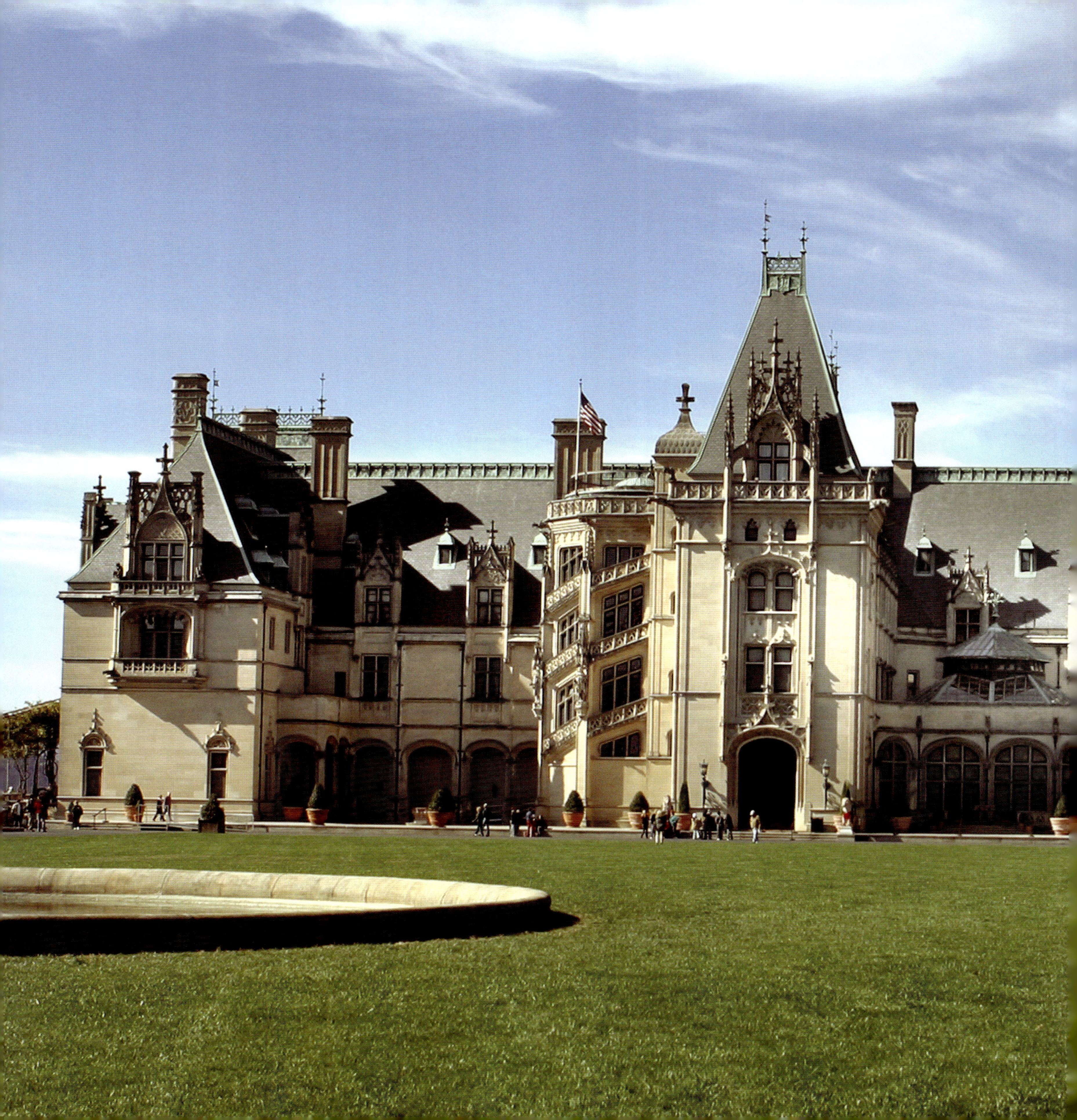

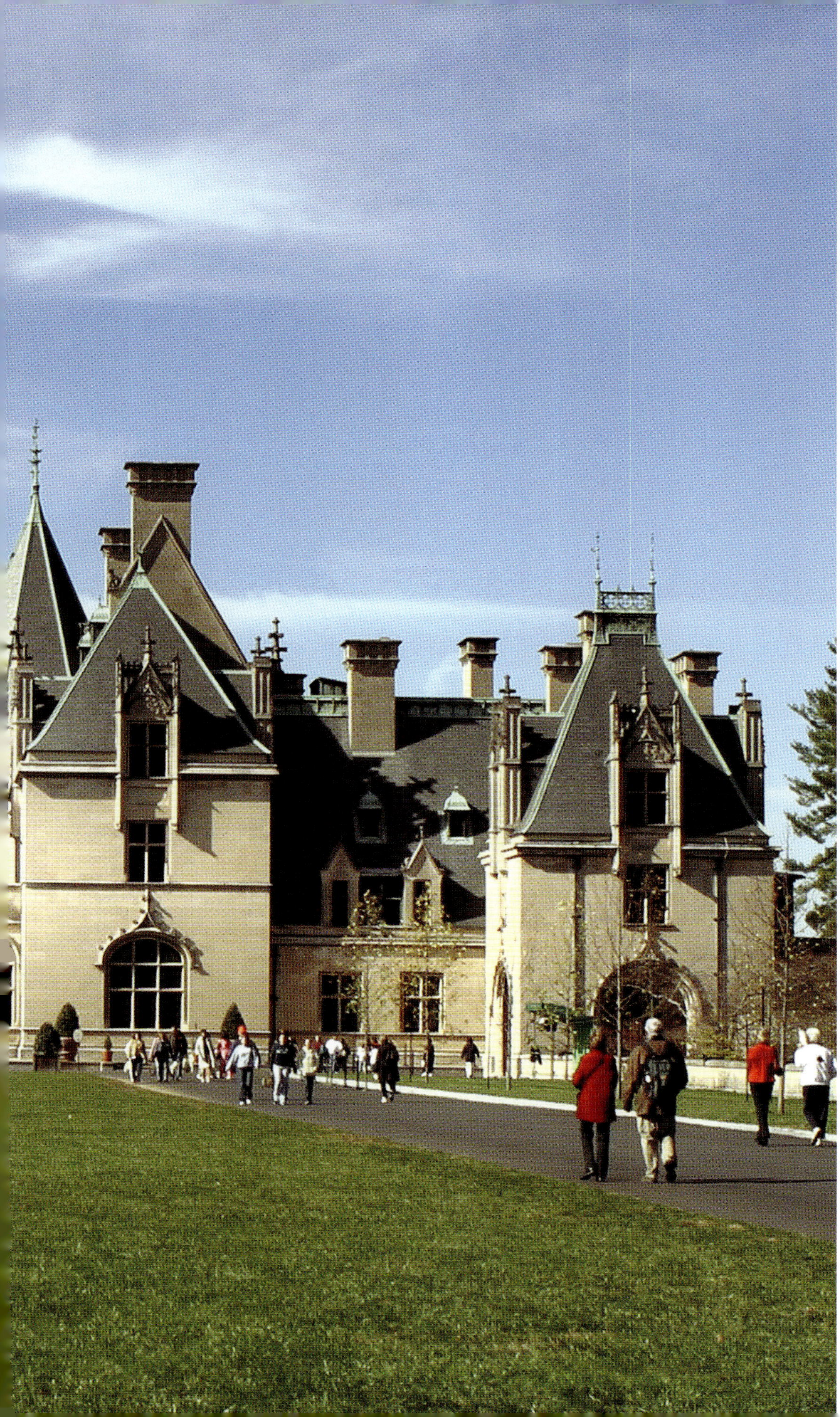

The Biltmore House is a chateau near Asheville. Built by George Washington Vanderbilt II between 1888 and 1895, it is the largest privately owned home in the United States, boasting 175,000 square feet. It is still owned by Vanderbilt's descendants, but is open to the public for tours.

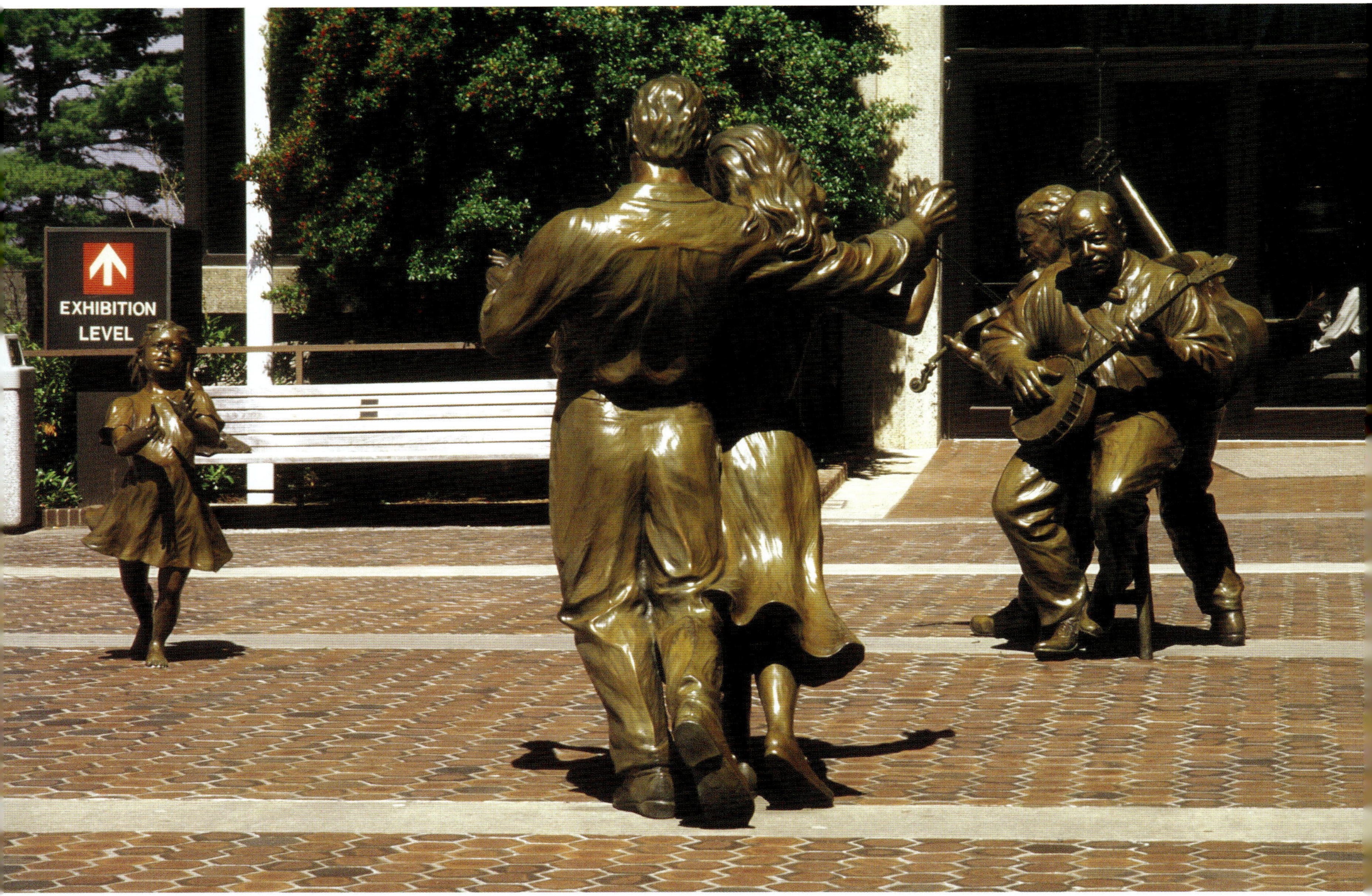

Outside the Asheville Civic Center, dancing figures seem to swing to the lively rhythms unique to the Appalachian Mountains. A regional destination for outstanding cultural and sporting events, the center is located in the heart of the vibrant entertainment district of downtown Asheville.

OPPOSITE PAGE: Dogwood and eastern redbud decorate the banks of one of many lakes near Asheville. Fishing and canoeing are available to those seeking peace and quiet.

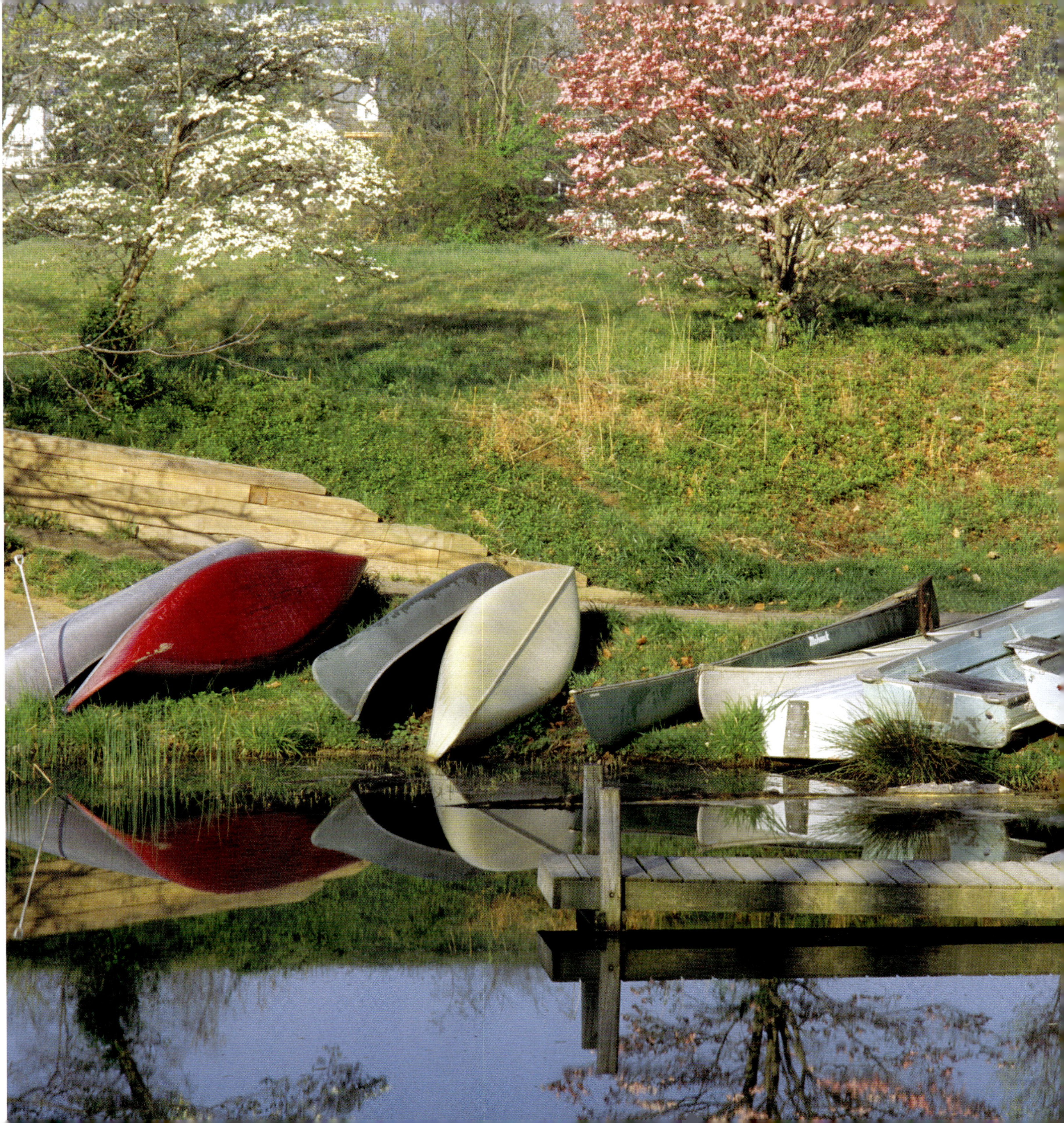

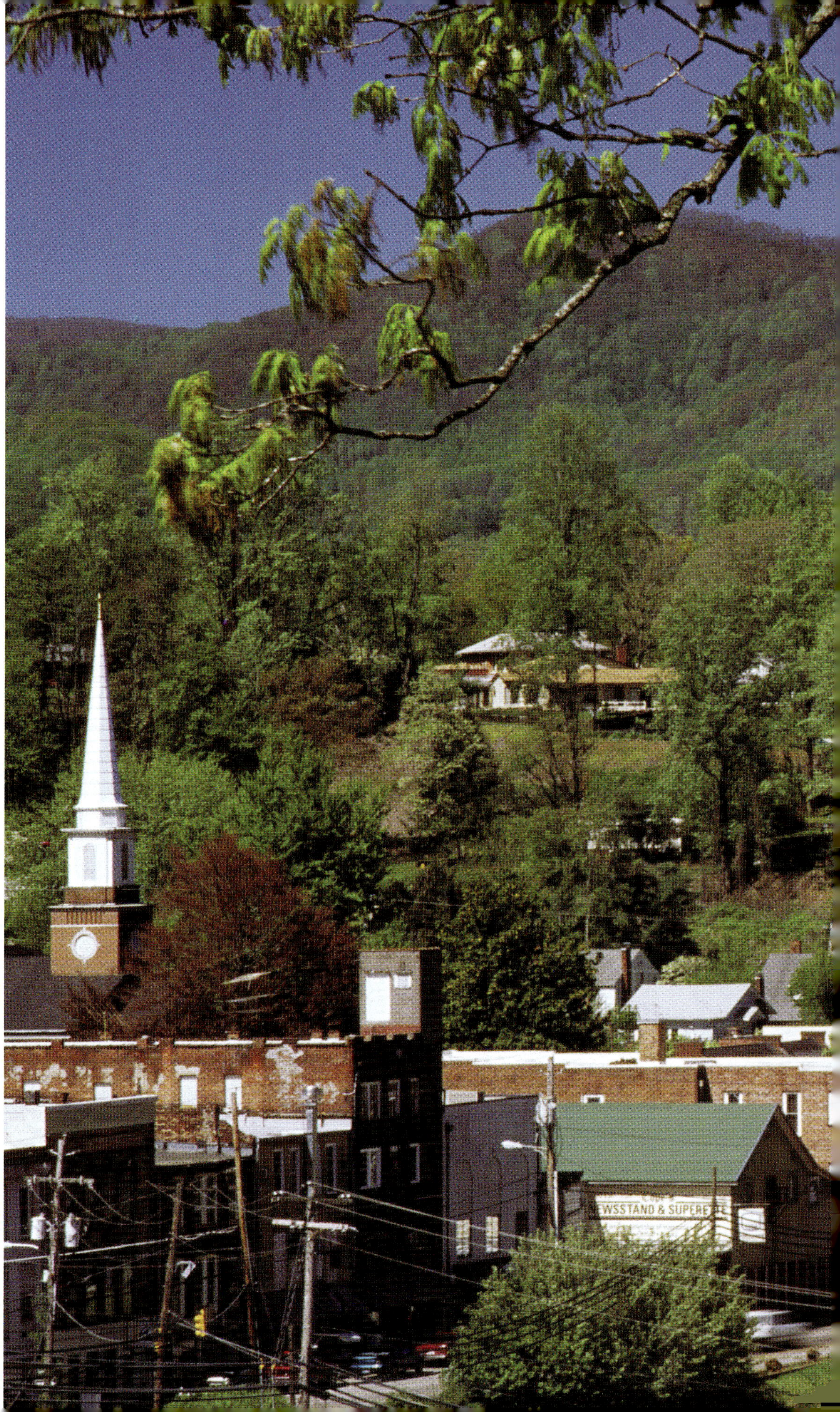

Old Jackson County Courthouse, built in 1914, looks down over the small town of Sylva as Kings Mountain rises in the background.

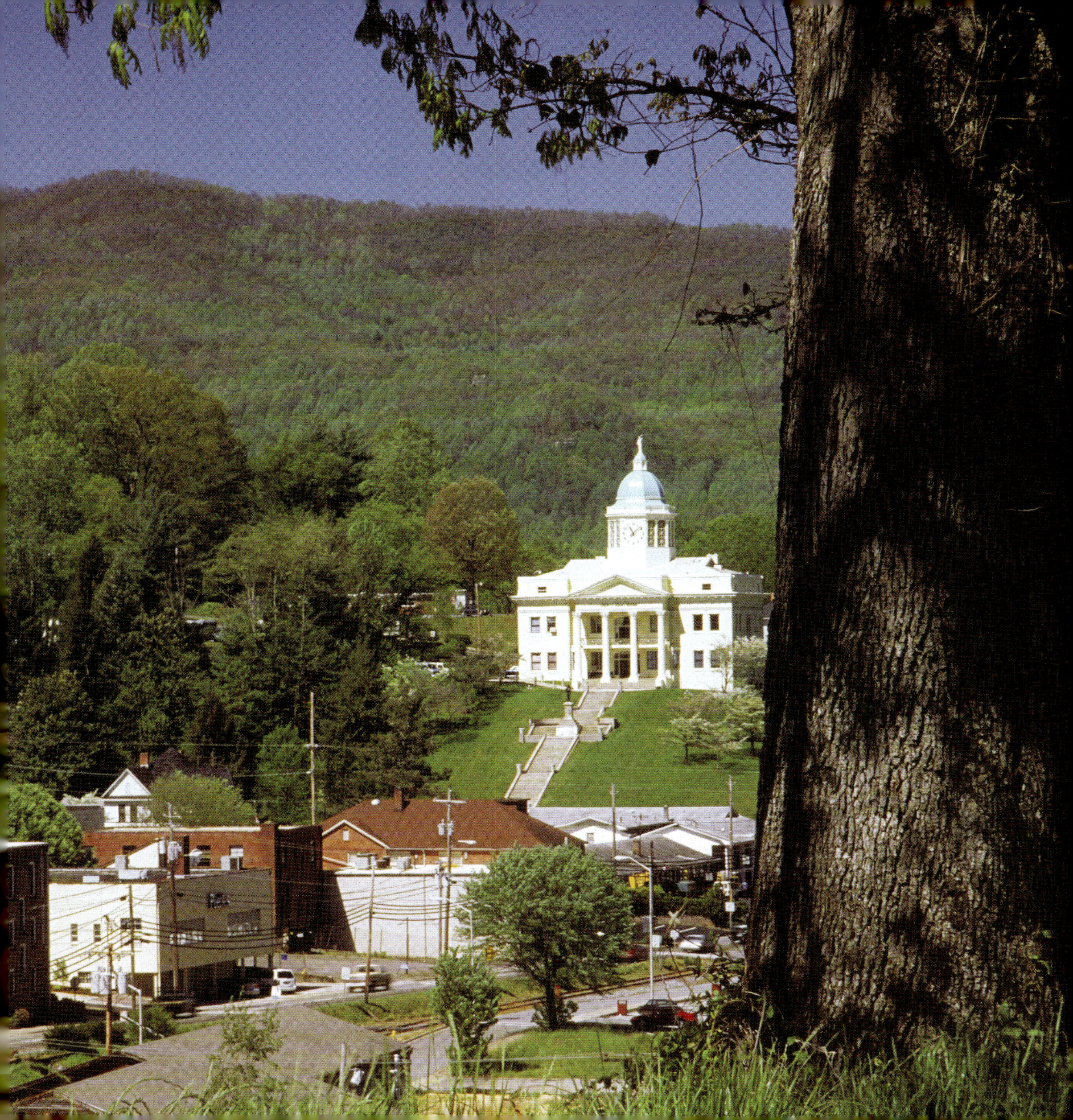

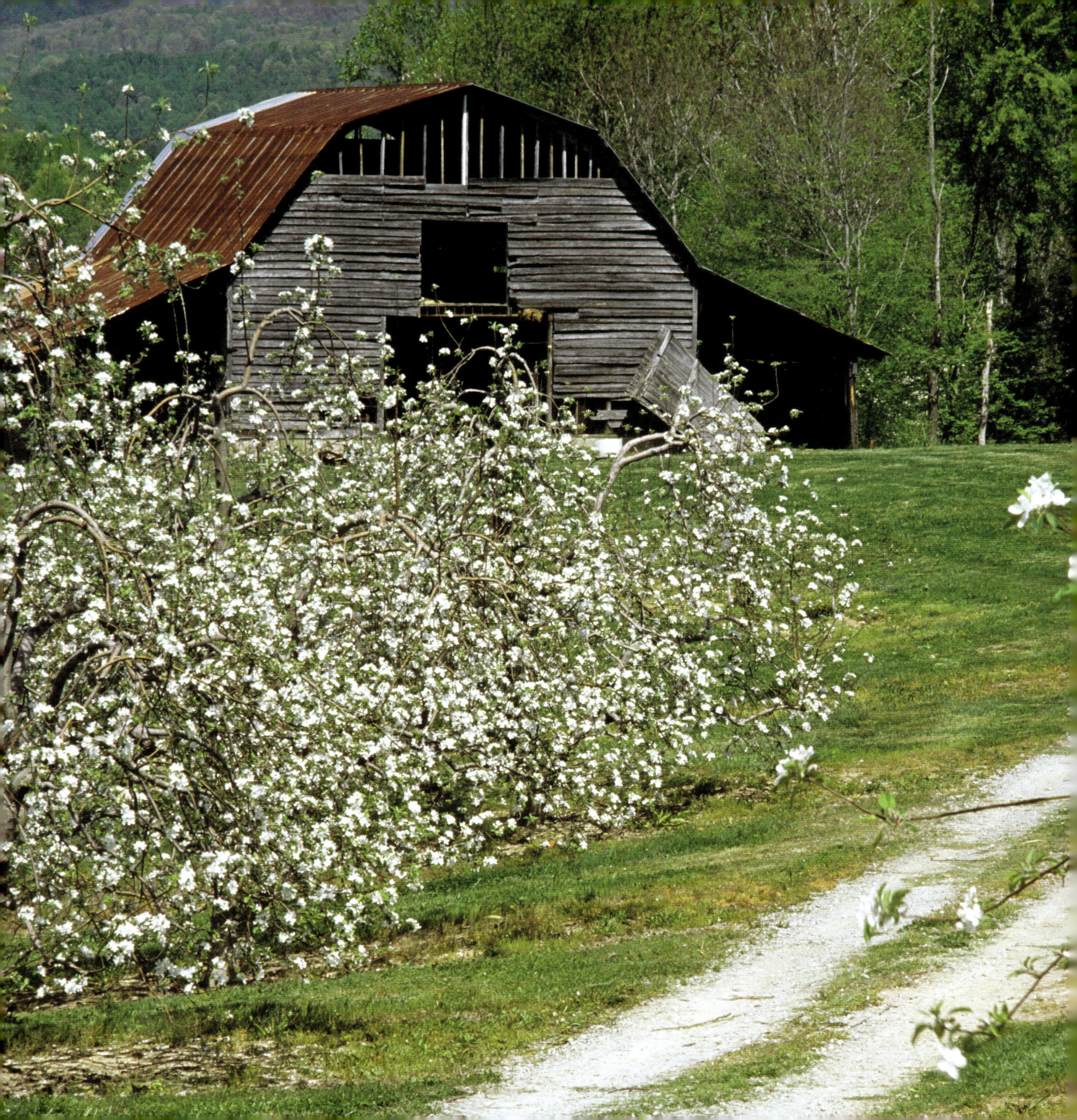

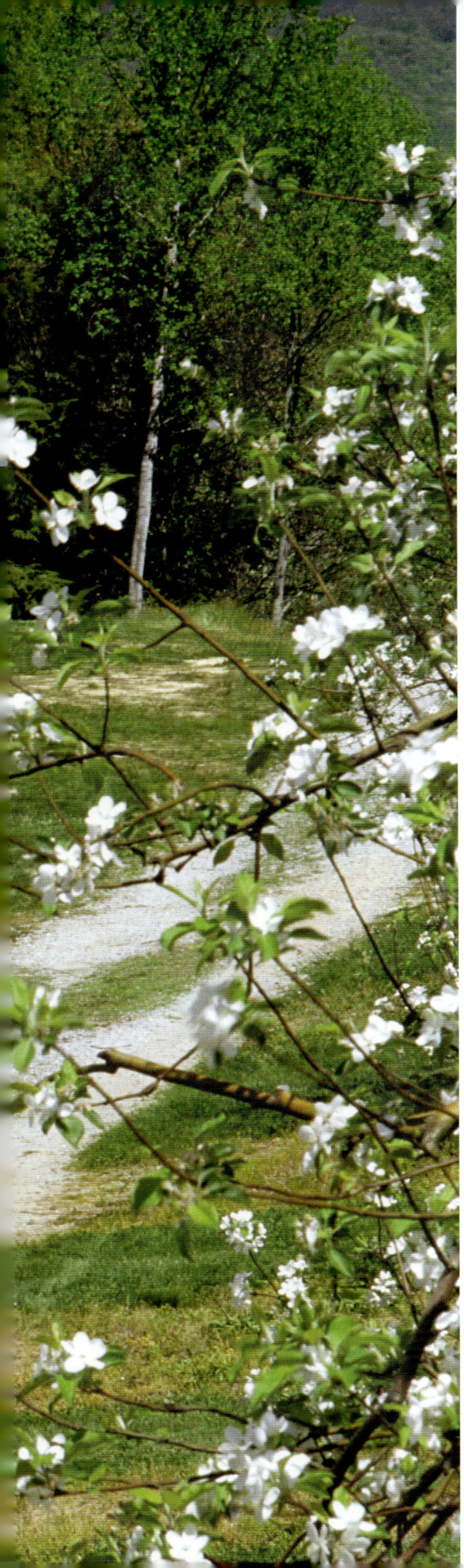

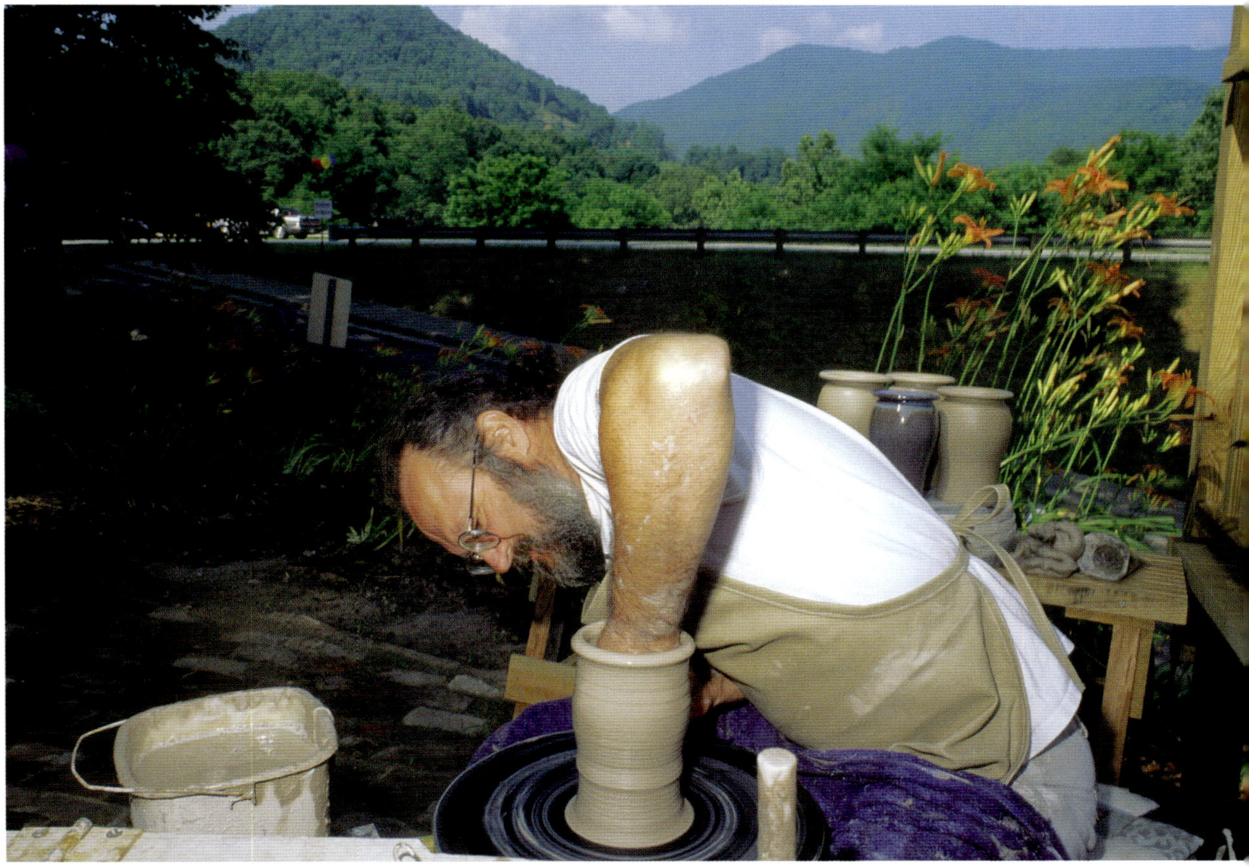

North Carolina artisans are famous for their craftsmanship. This potter works near Cold Mountain, the focal point for the best-selling novel and popular movie of the same name.

LEFT: North Carolina is the nation's seventh largest apple producer, and Henderson County is the largest producer in the state. In spring, the county is a mass of orchards in bloom. In fall, apples and cider may be purchased from one of the many picturesque roadside stands.

FOLLOWING PAGE: Framed by a profusion of wild rhododendrons, the view toward Middle Prong Wilderness can be seen from the Blue Ridge Parkway. With intentionally few amenities, it remains a safe haven for a diverse range of native plants and animals.

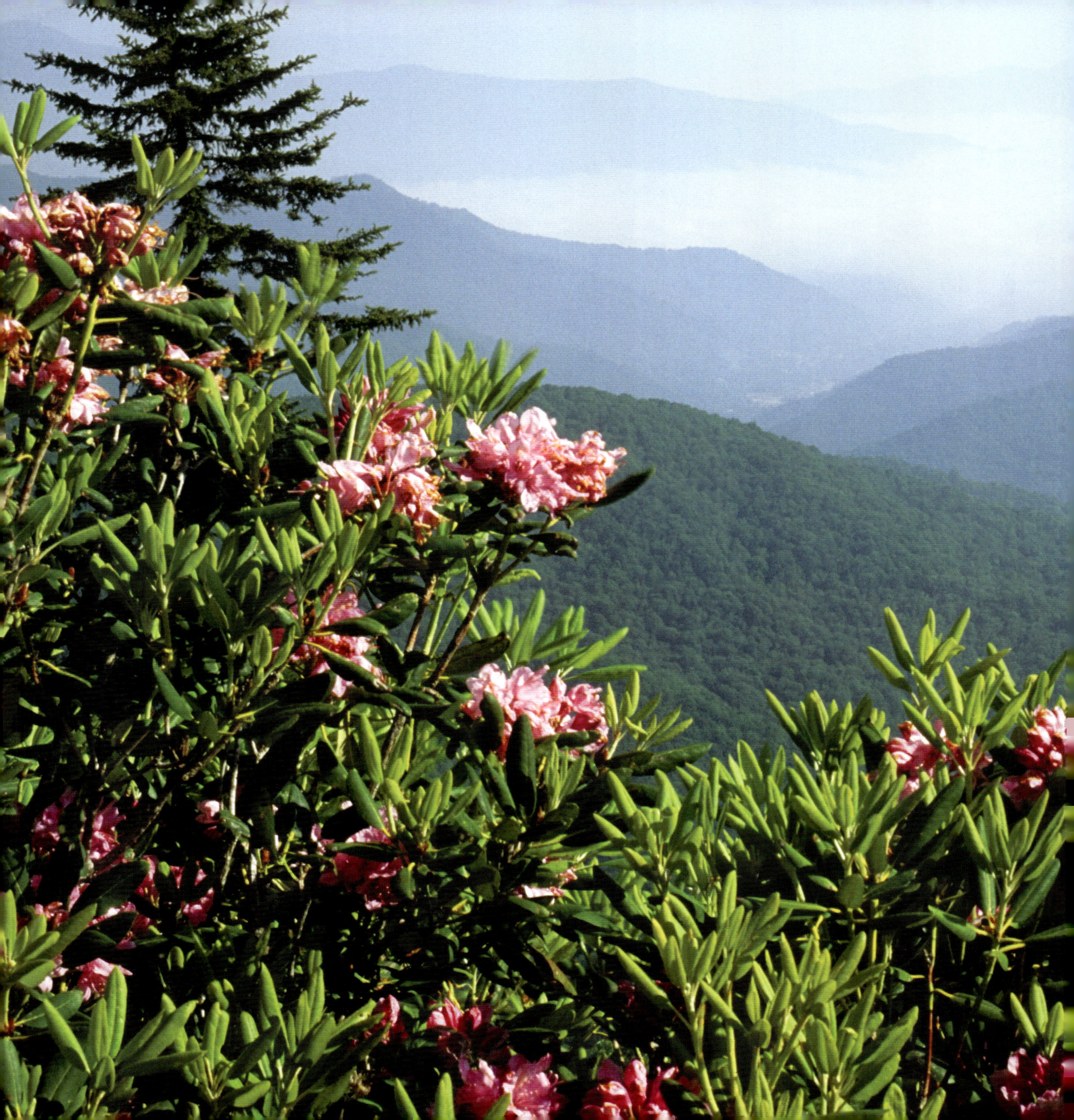

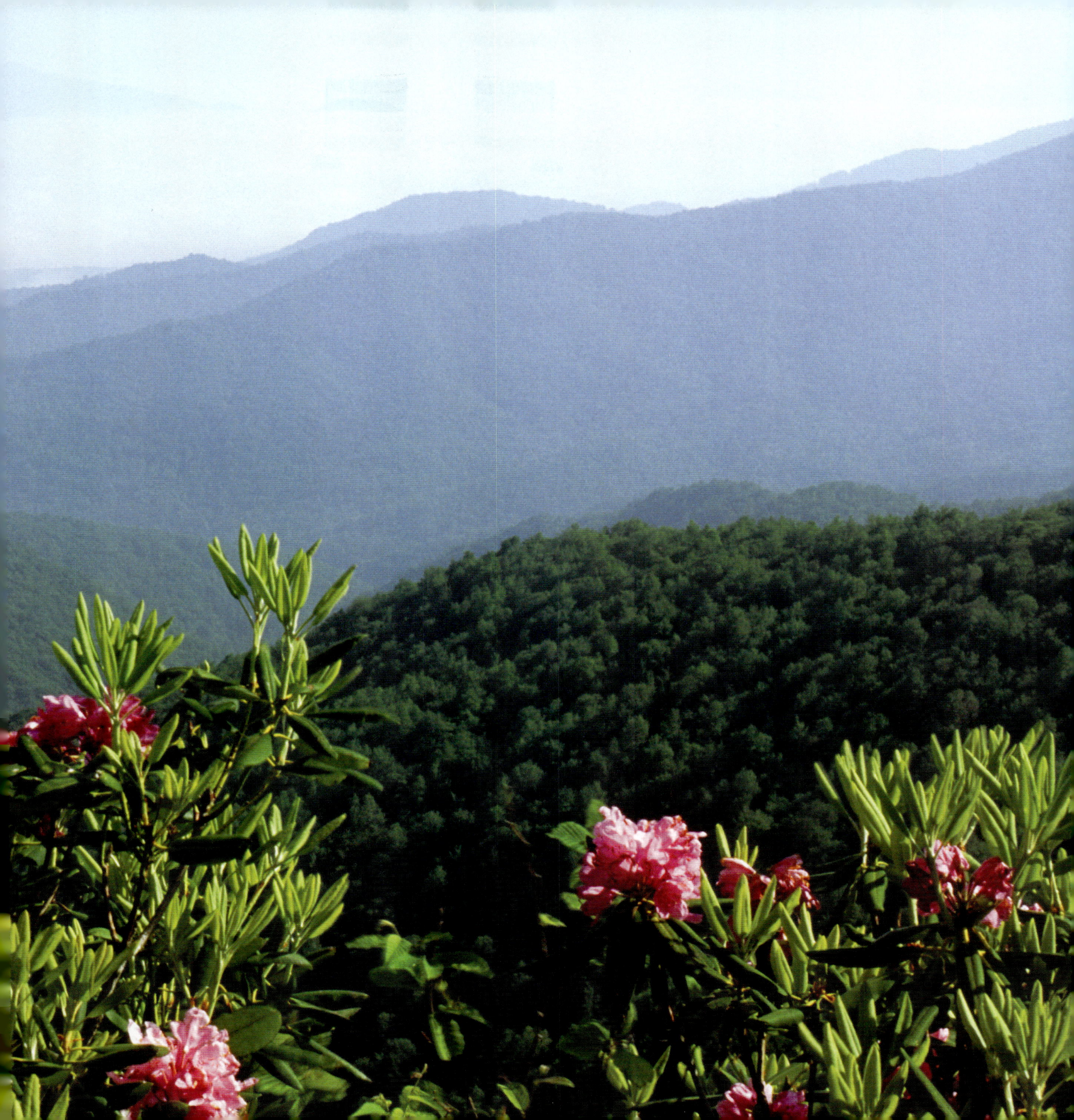

The sunrise softens the fall fog in the early morning, looking down from Fry Mountain. Much of this land is in the Qualla Boundary, which is the proper name for the Cherokee Indian Reservation.

OPPOSITE PAGE: The dome of Looking Glass Rock gets its name from the thin coatings of ice that sometimes build up to reflect the winter light after a freezing rain. The rock has several faces to challenge any climber, from amateur to expert.

FOLLOWING PAGE: The Devil's Courthouse is a large overhang on Whiteside Mountain near the North Carolina–Georgia border. Rising out of the Nantahala Forest, this massive granite formation is between 390 and 460 million years old. The sides of the mountain look like sheets of ice and have long served as a landmark along the Eastern Continental Divide.

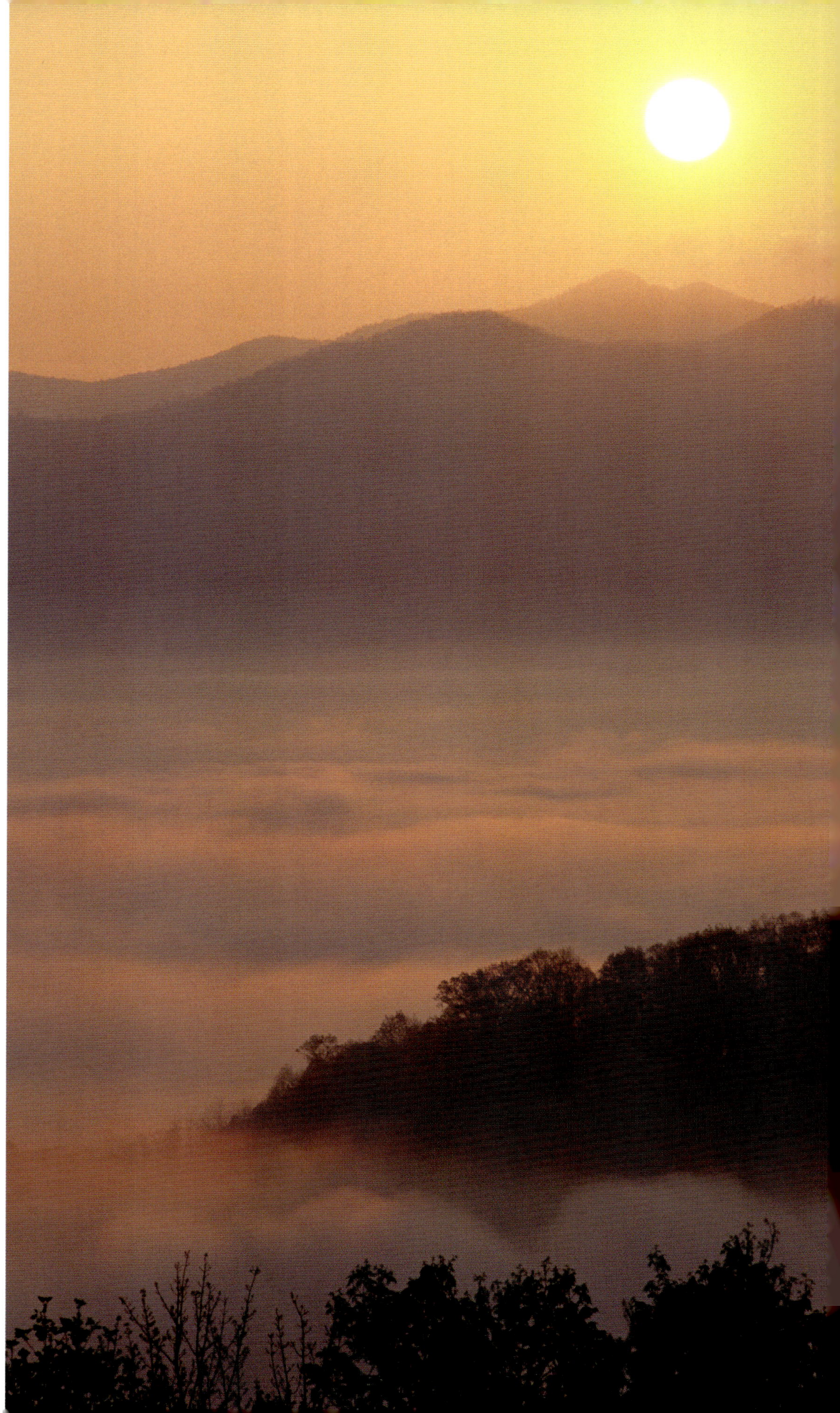

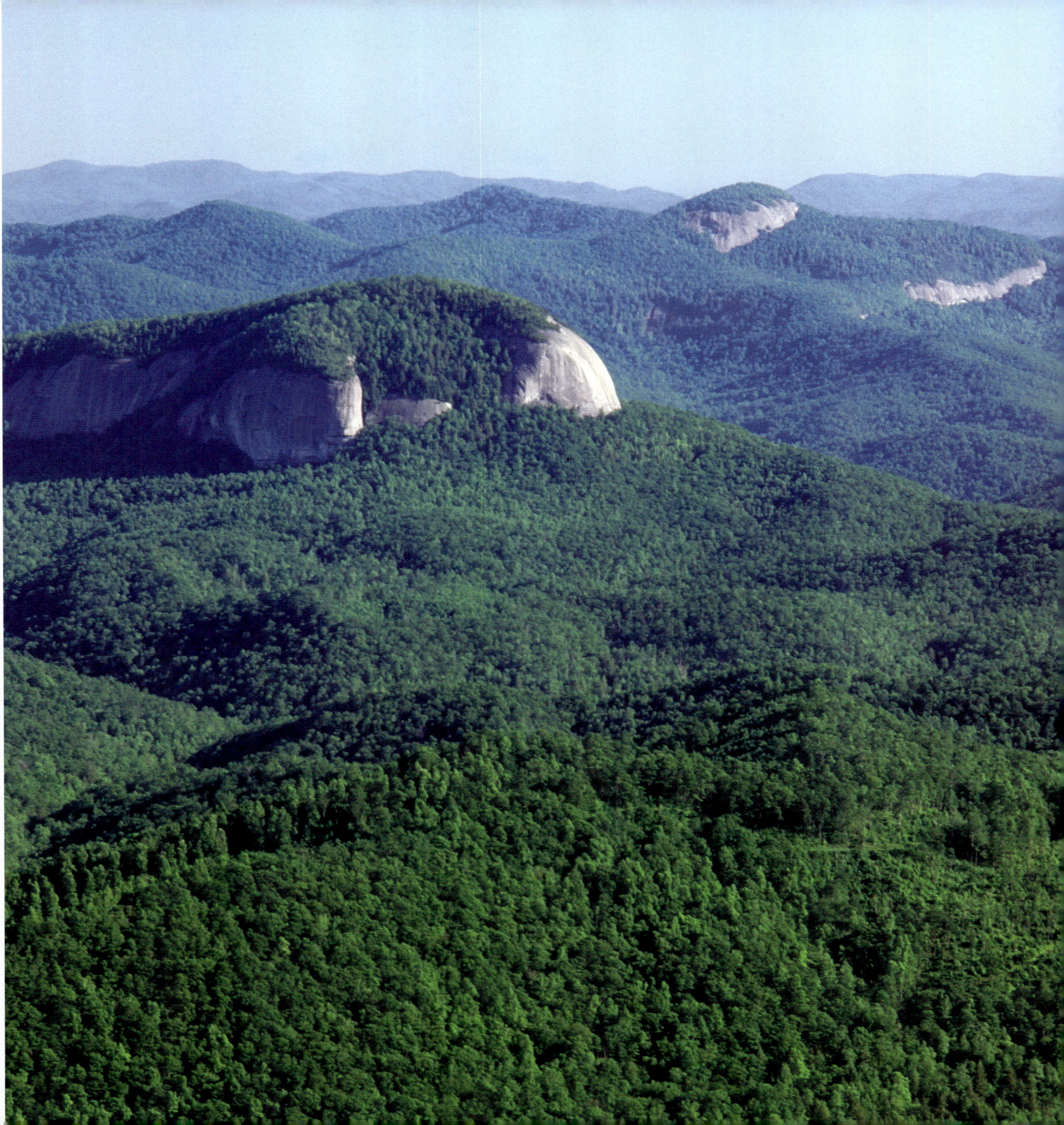

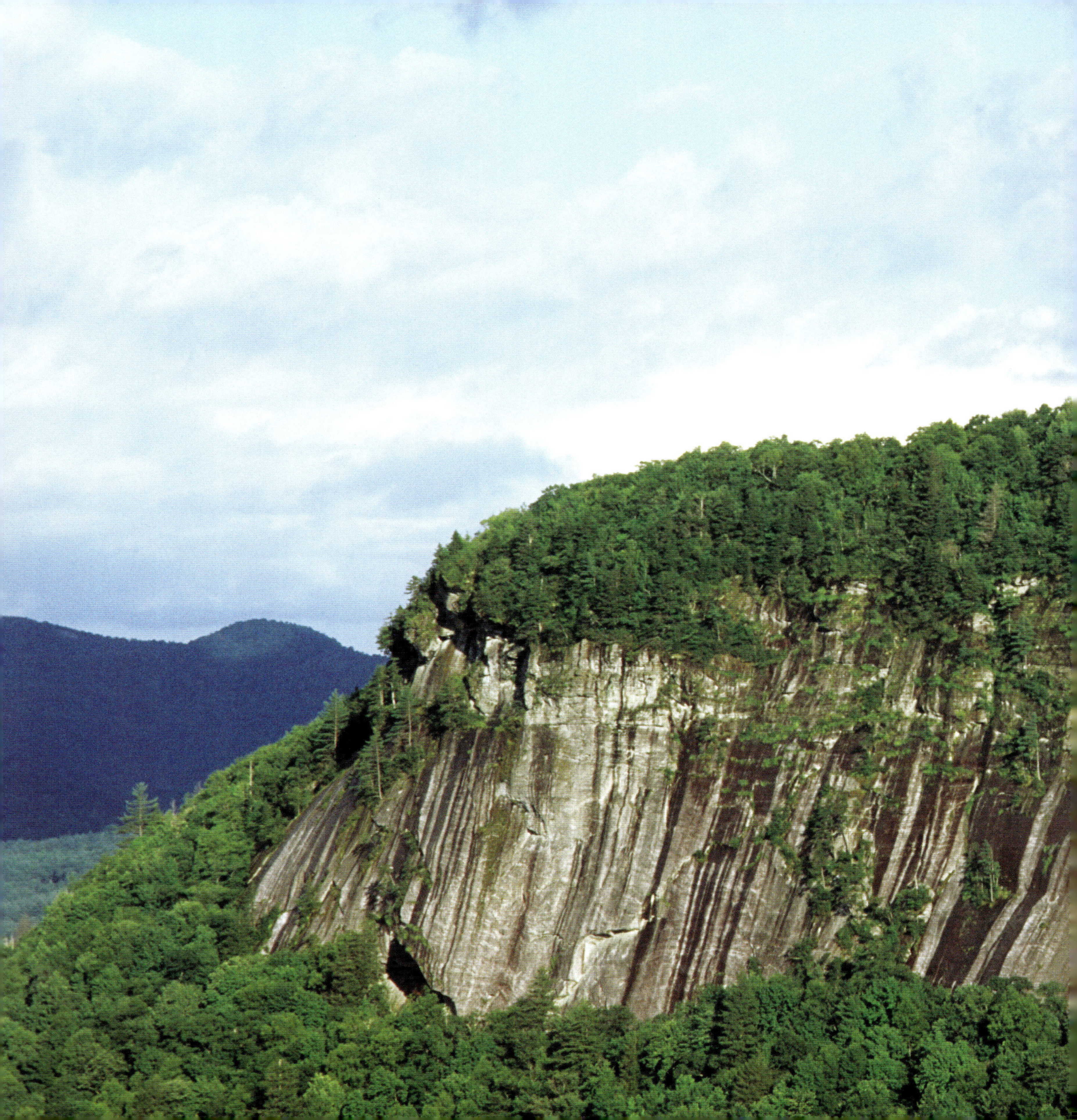

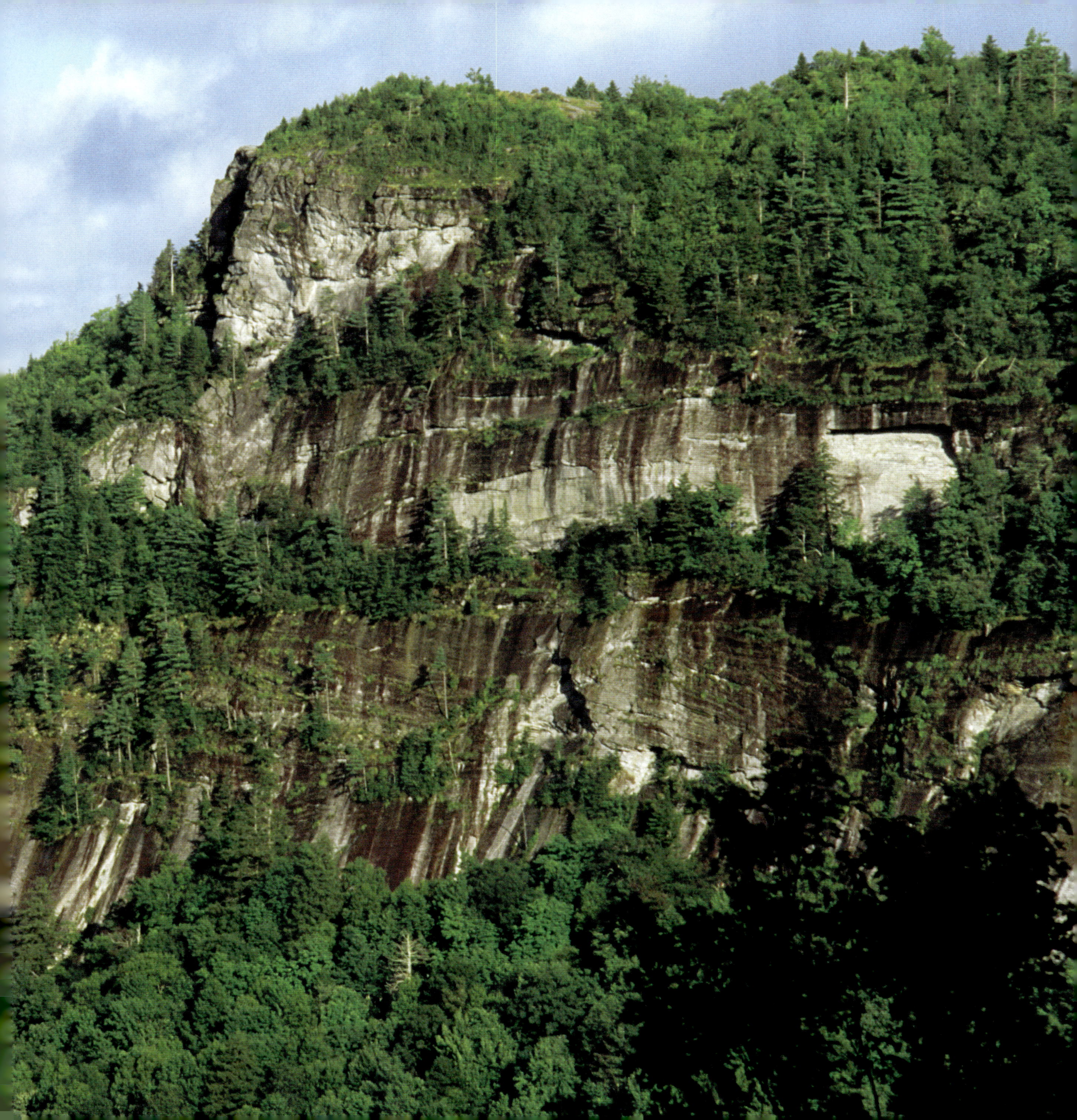

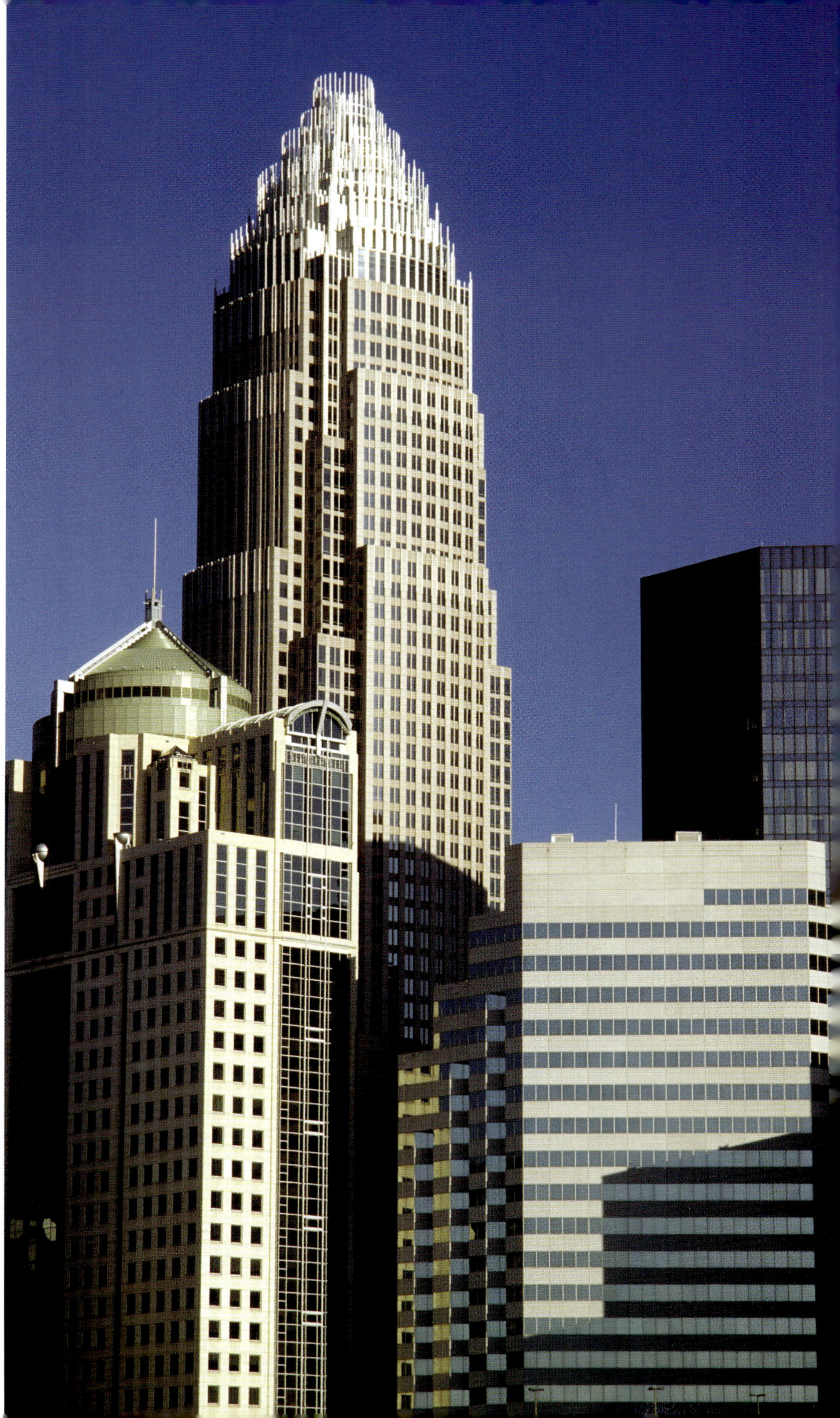

The modern architecture of downtown Charlotte reflects the dynamic city core, alive with theaters, fine restaurants, concert halls and conference centers. The Piedmont Region in the central part of the state includes six of North Carolina's largest cities.

OPPOSITE PAGE: The neighborhood of Myers Park is one of Charlotte's most prestigious residential areas. The area is famous for the imposing trees that line its curving streets.

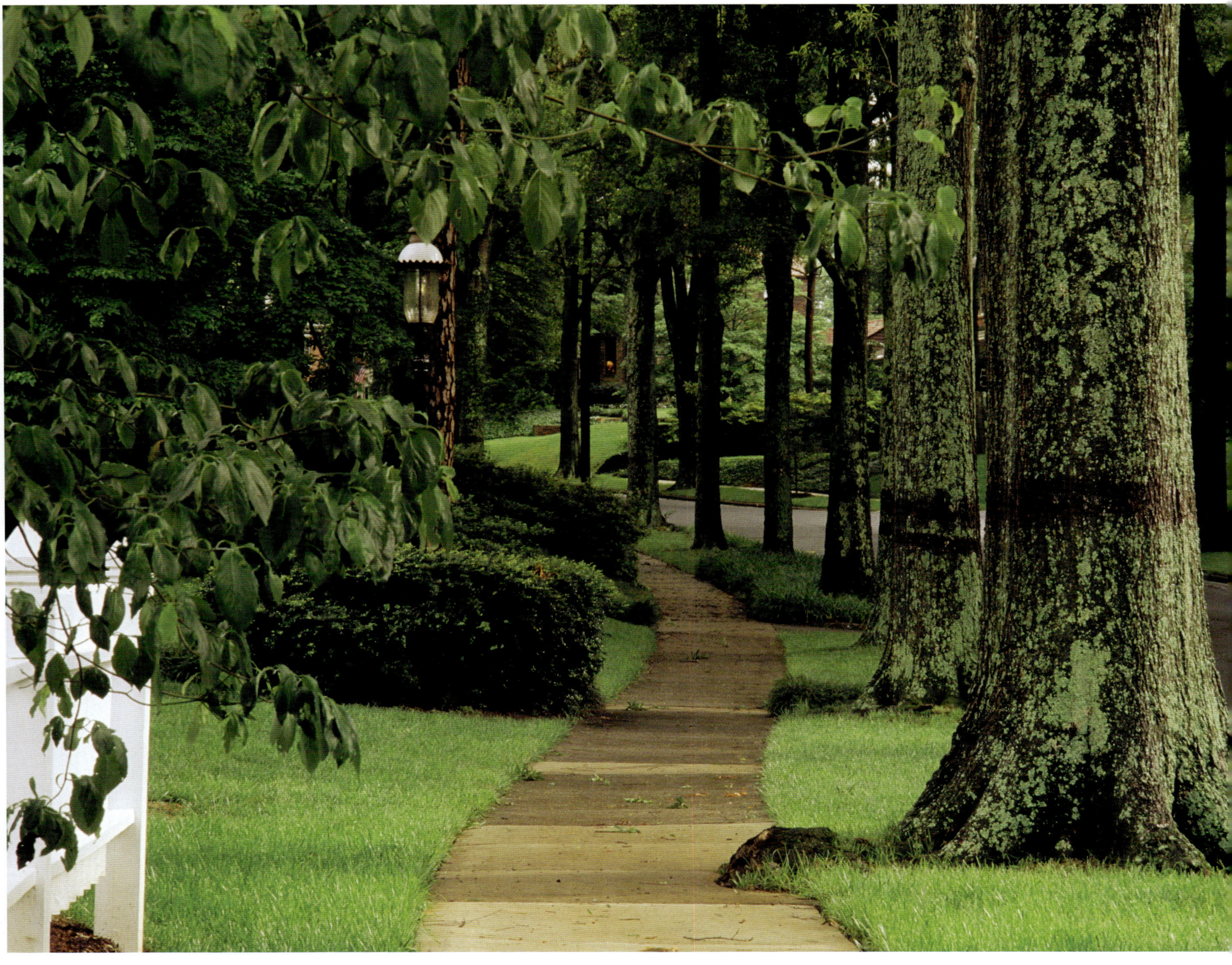

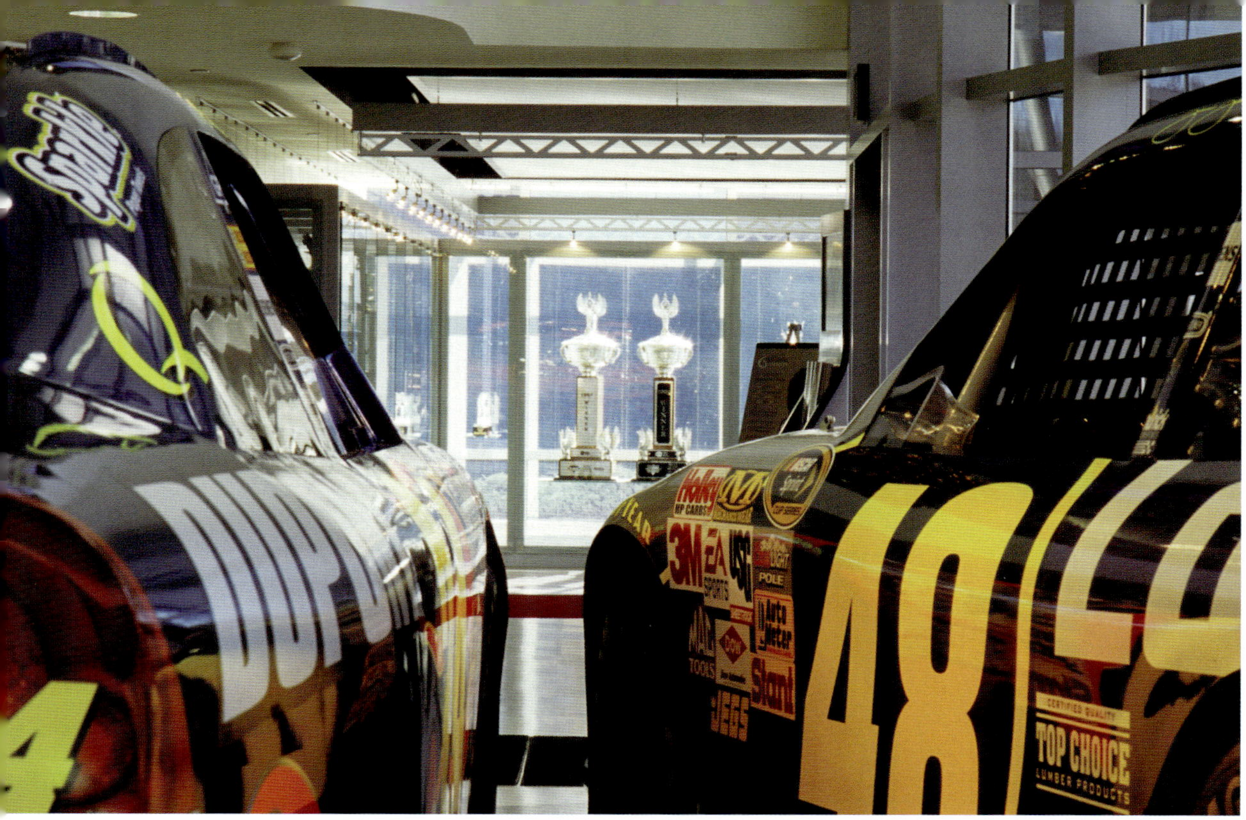

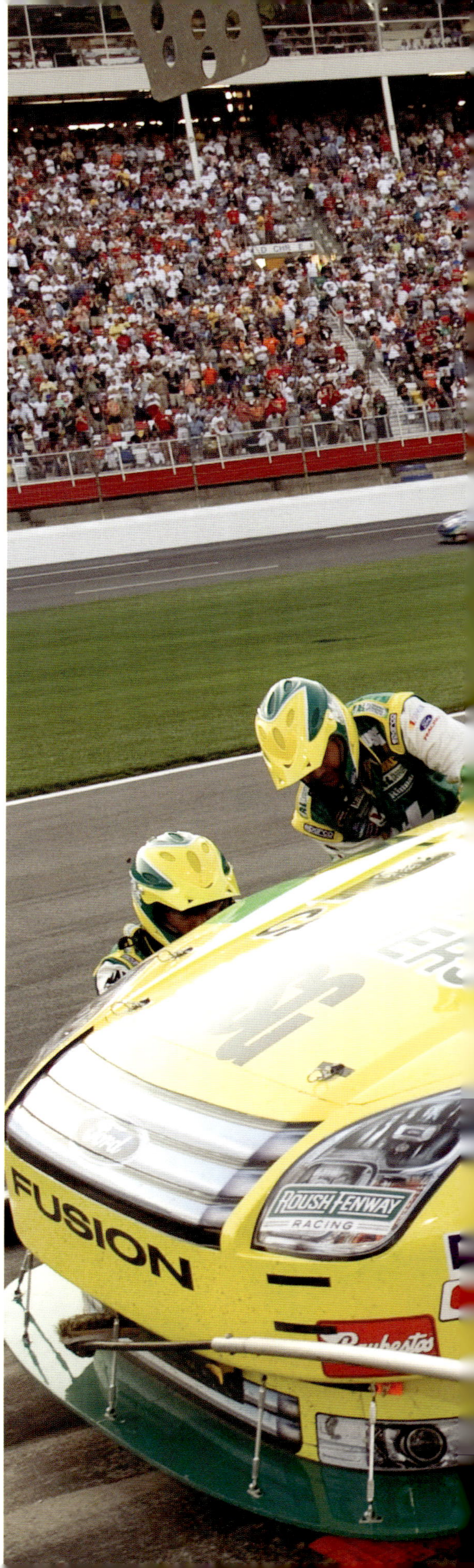

Stock car racing is a North Carolina tradition, and the state is the birthplace of many NASCAR legends, including Dale Earnhardt and Richard Petty. The Hendrick Motorsports racing complex (above), where NASCAR-winning stock cars are on display, is located in Charlotte. Lowe's Motor Speedway (right), just outside the city, hosts major races – including three NASCAR Winston Cup events – each year on its 1.5-mile superspeedway.

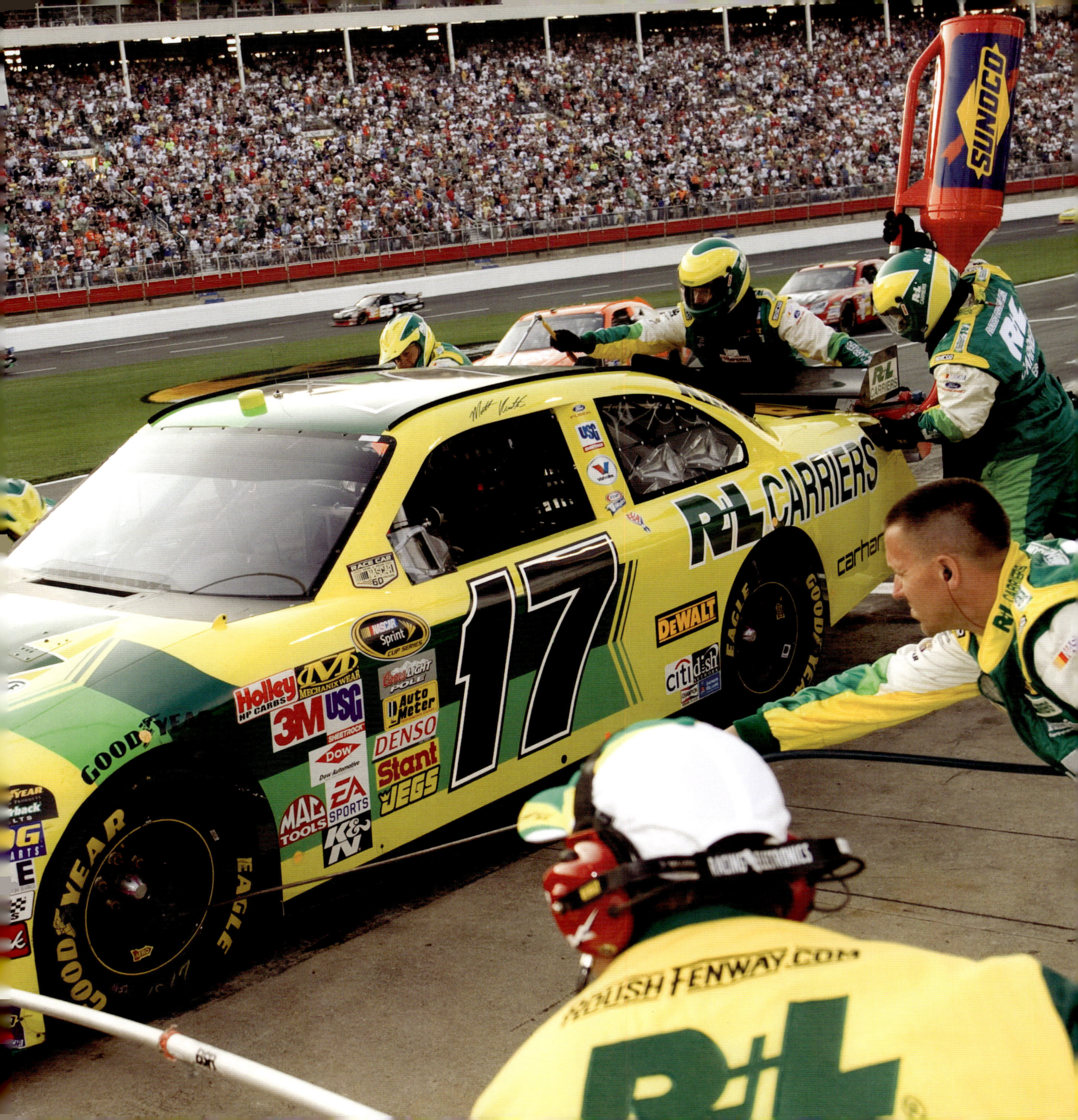
SUNOCO
R+L CARRIERS
17
DEWALT
Holley
HP CARBS
MECHANIX WEAR
3M
USG
DOW
DENSO
Stant
JEGS
MAC TOOLS
EA SPORTS
K&N
Auto Meter
GOODYEAR
EAGLE
ROUSHFENWAY.COM
R+L

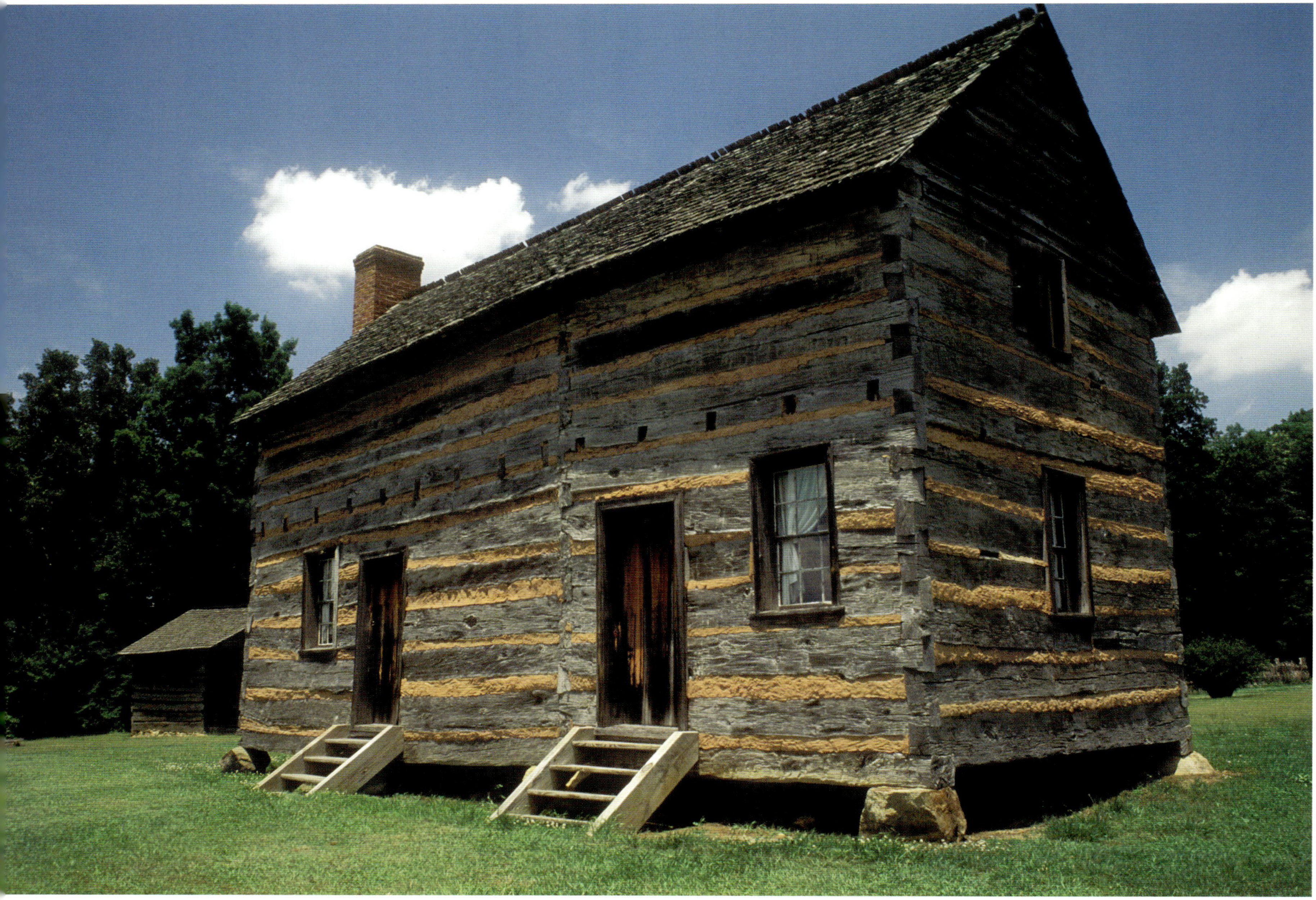

Pineville, North Carolina, just southwest of Charlotte, is the birthplace and childhood home of the 11th U.S. President, James K. Polk. This reconstructed log cabin sits on land once owned by the president's parents. It is now a state historic site and provides a glimpse into life during the early 19th century.

OPPOSITE PAGE: An explosion of orchards in bloom announce the arrival of spring across the state. With its diversity of products – tobacco and yams, hogs, Christmas trees, turkeys and fruit – it ranks eight nationally in farm income.

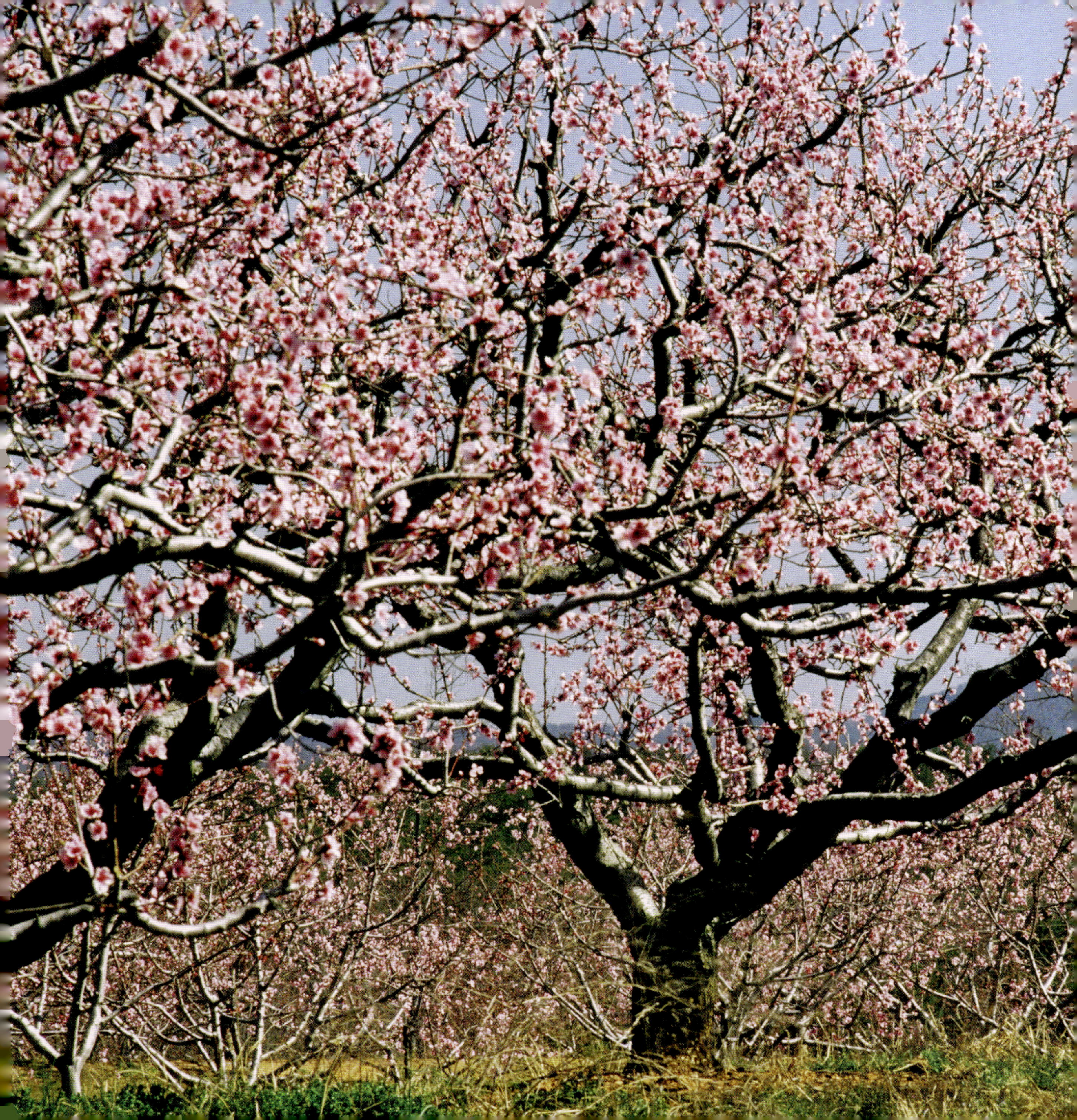

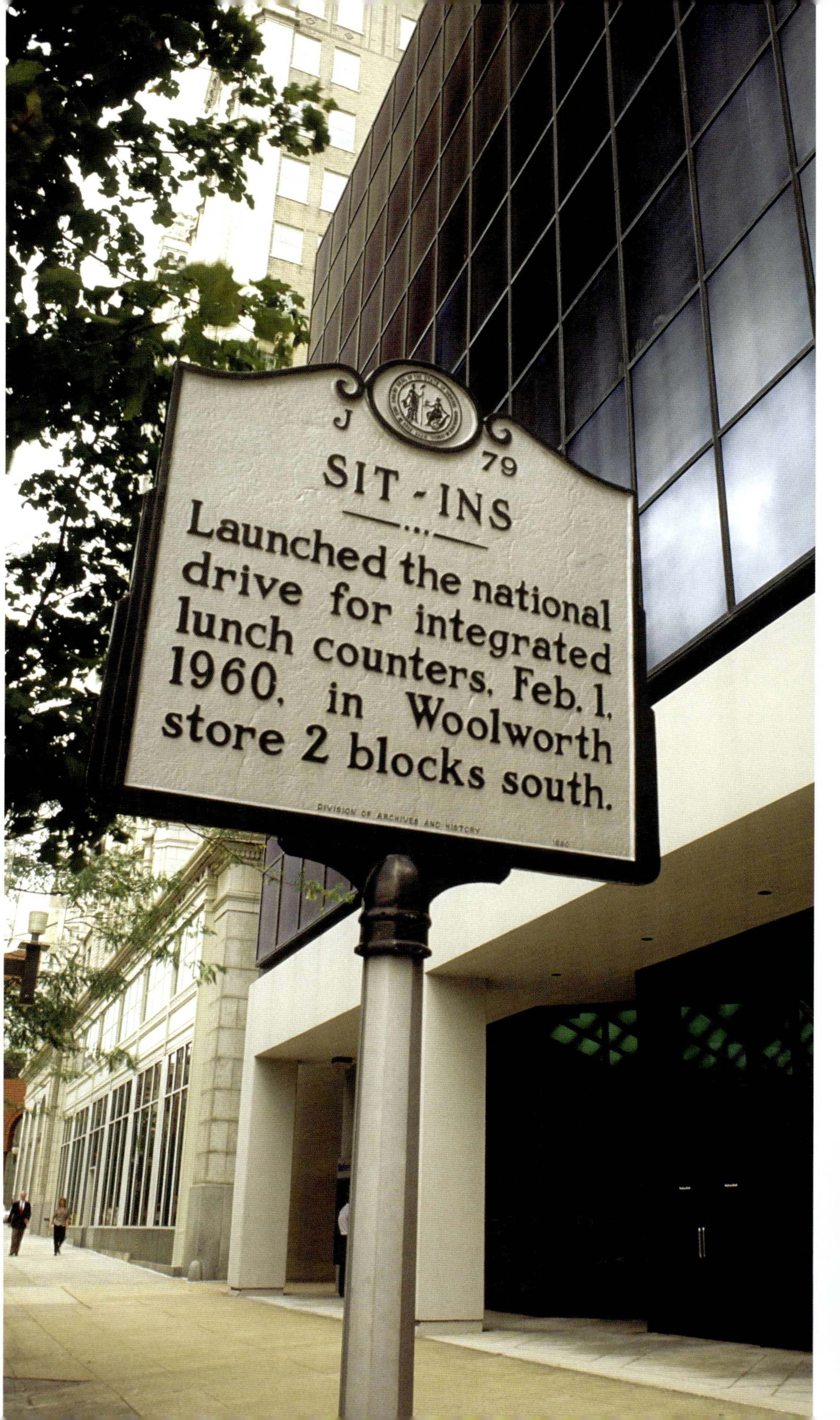

On February 1, 1960, civil rights participants staged a sit-in for racial equality at the lunch counter of Woolworth's Department Store in Greensboro. This specific action served as an example for non-violent protests across the nation. The Greensboro Historical Museum features displays of the lunch counter sit-ins, along with other exhibits of the region's history.

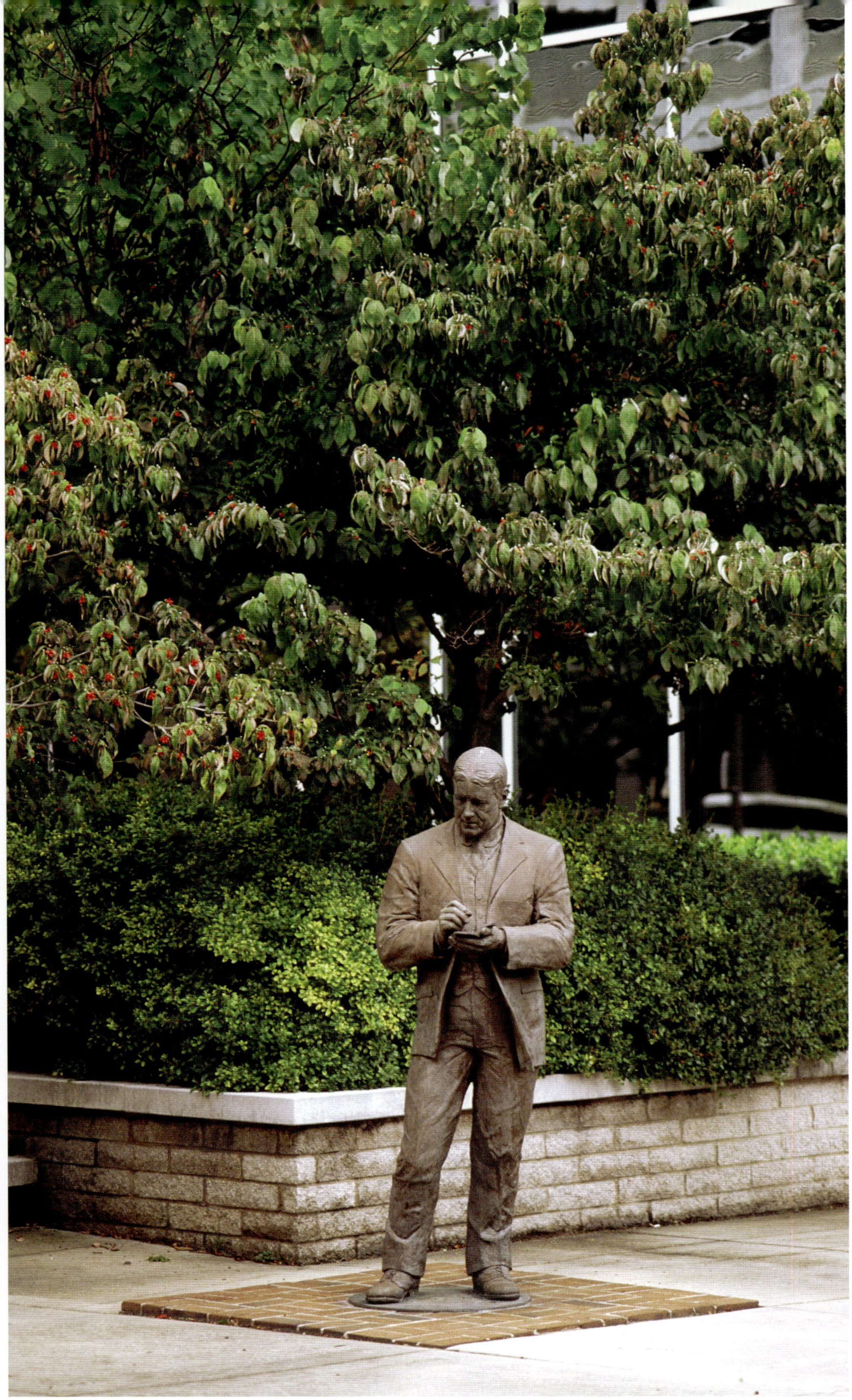

Bronze sculptures in downtown Greensboro pay tribute to one of America's favorite short story writers. O. Henry, who was a master of surprise endings, was born William Sydney Porter in Greensboro, in 1862.

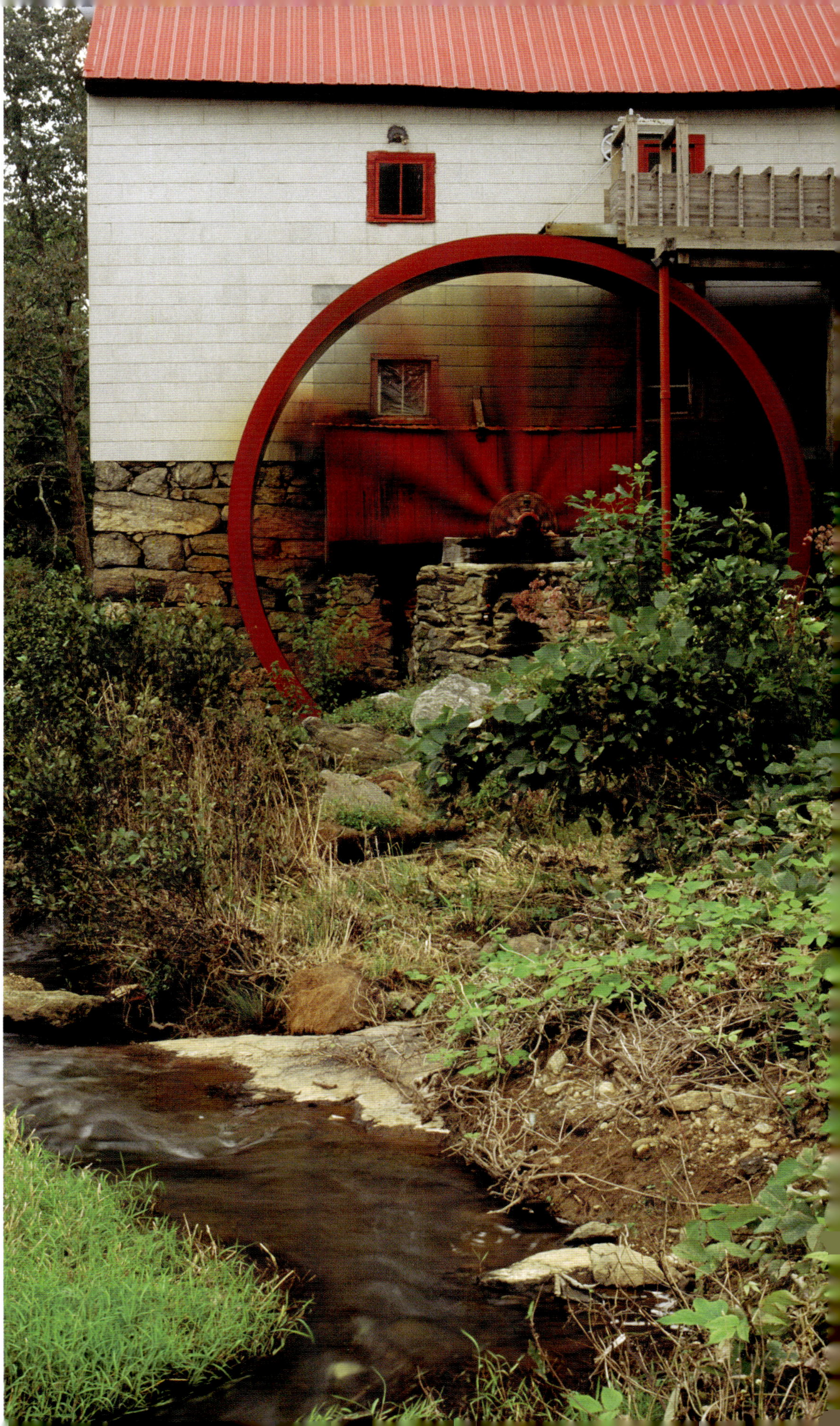

The Old Mill of Guilford, west of Greensboro, dates from 1767, when it was used for grinding grain for the early settlers. Although the original waterwheel has been replaced, the mill is still in full operation.

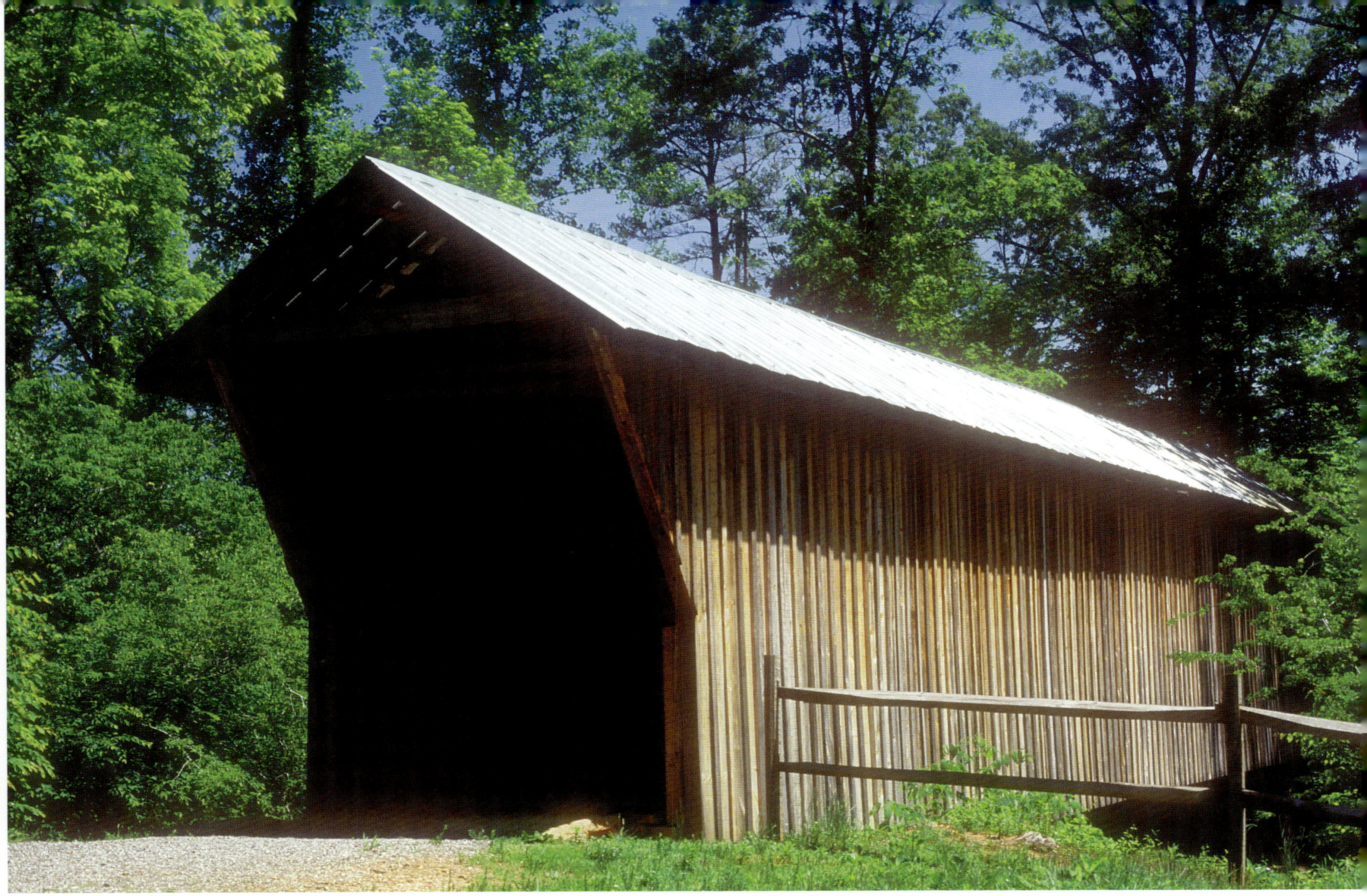

The Bunker Hill Covered Bridge over Lyle Creek was built in 1895. The design was based on a patent by the Civil War General Herman Haupt and has been designated a National Civil Engineering Landmark.

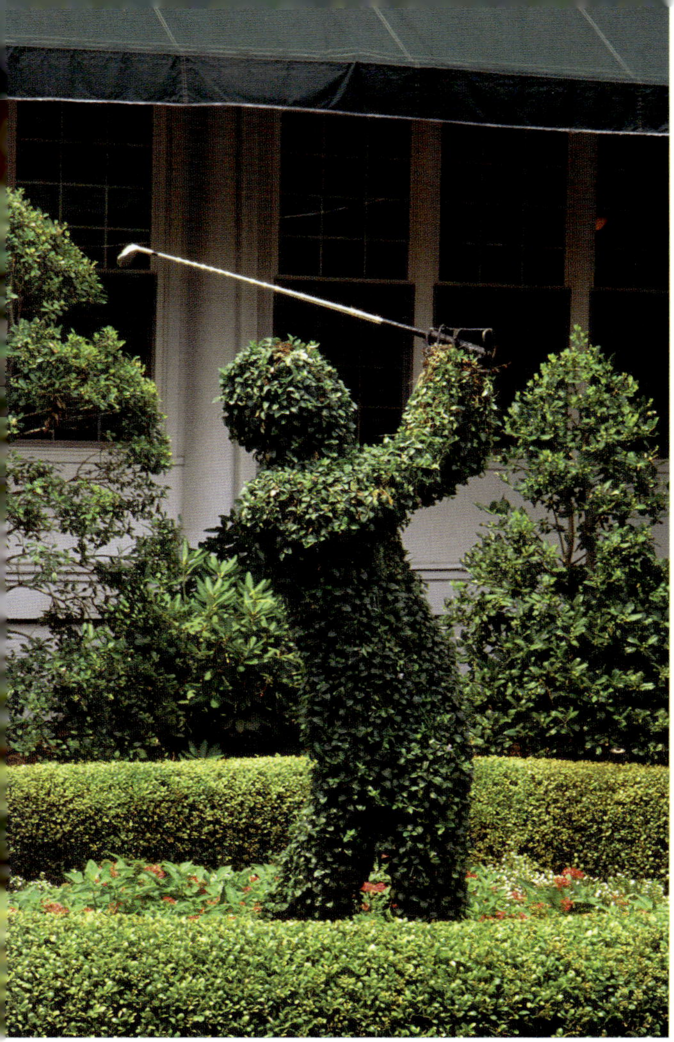

This topiary "Putter Boy" represents North Carolina's passion for golf. Hundreds of courses weave their way through the varied landscapes of the state, offering some of the most picturesque fairways in the world.

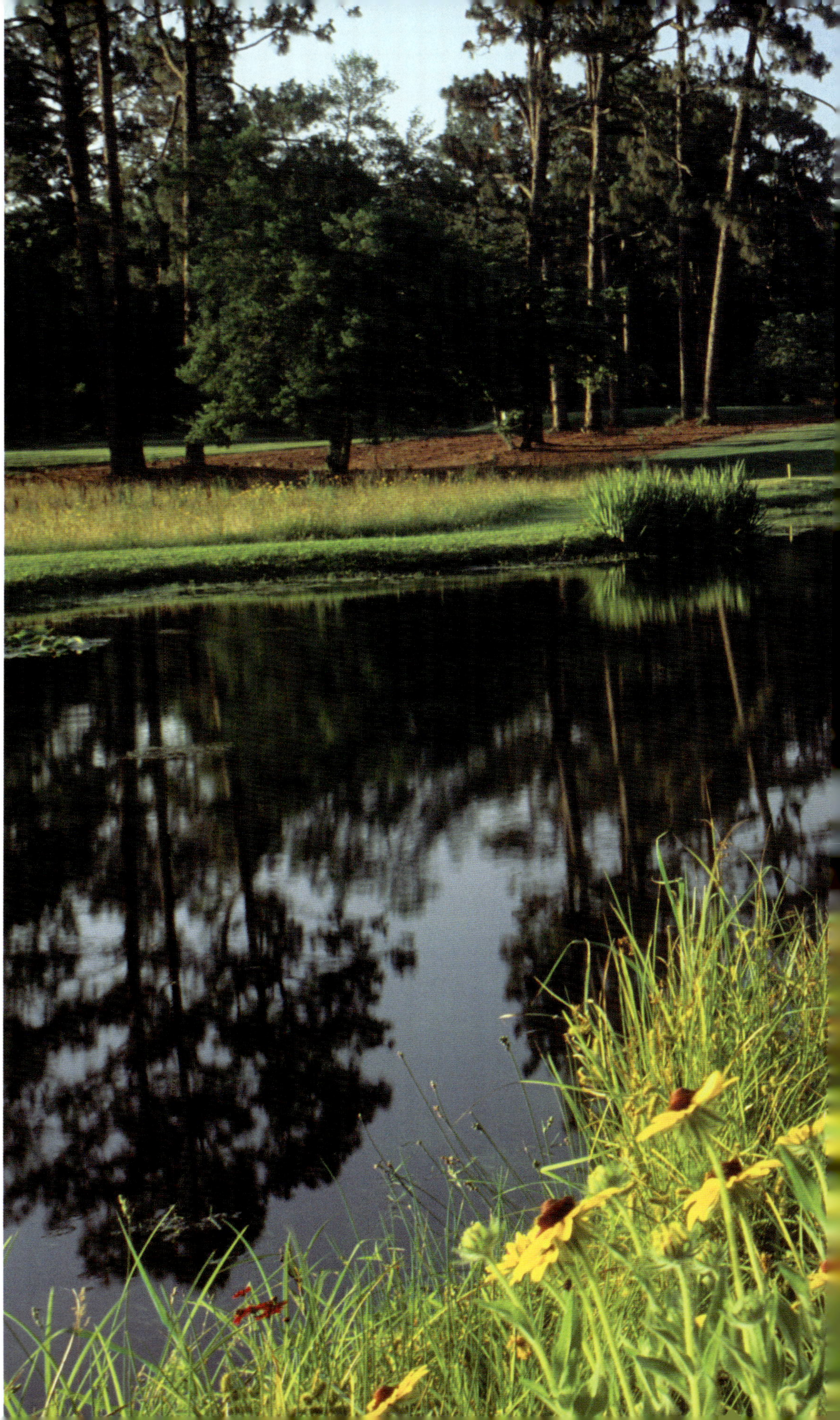

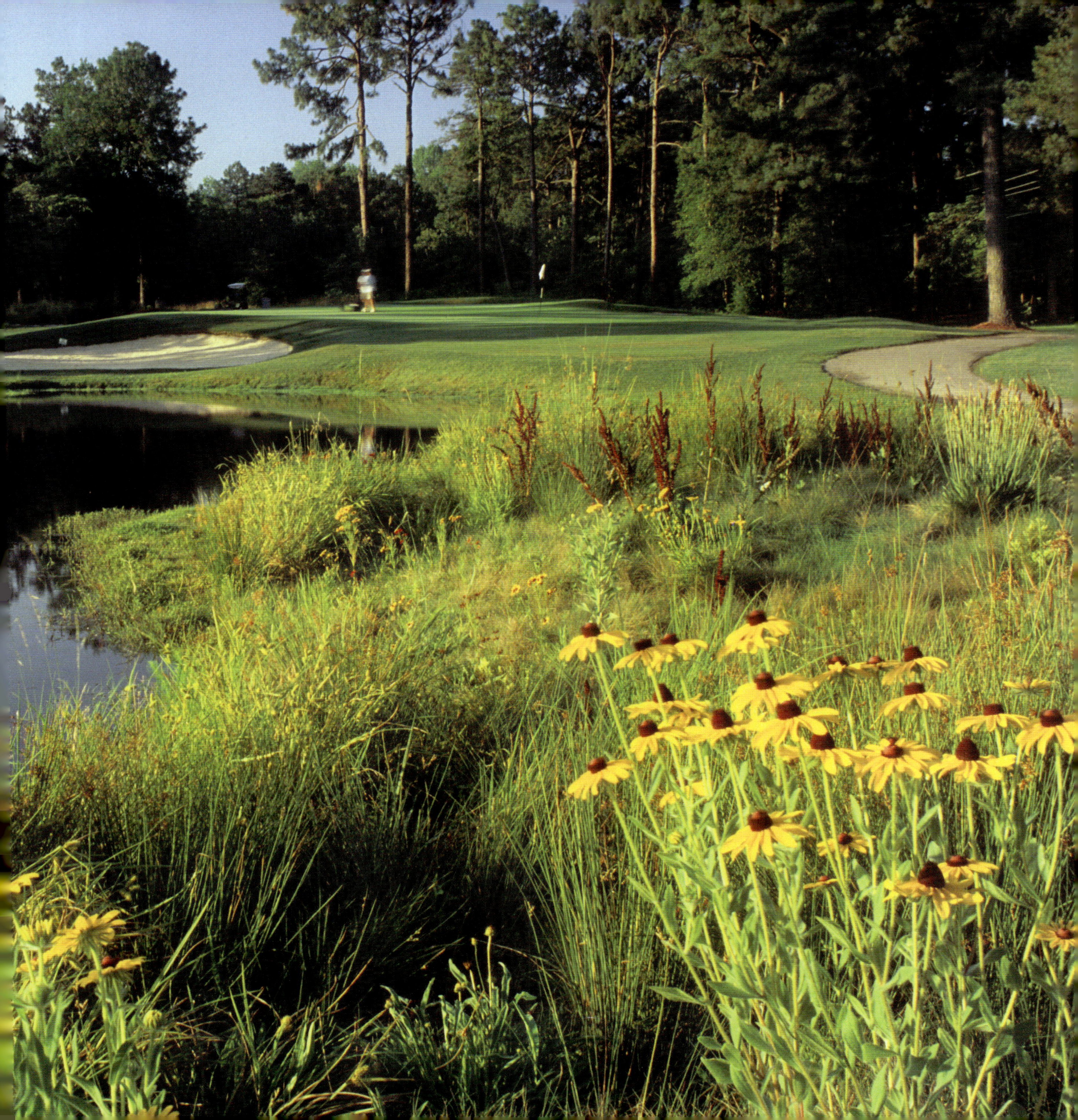

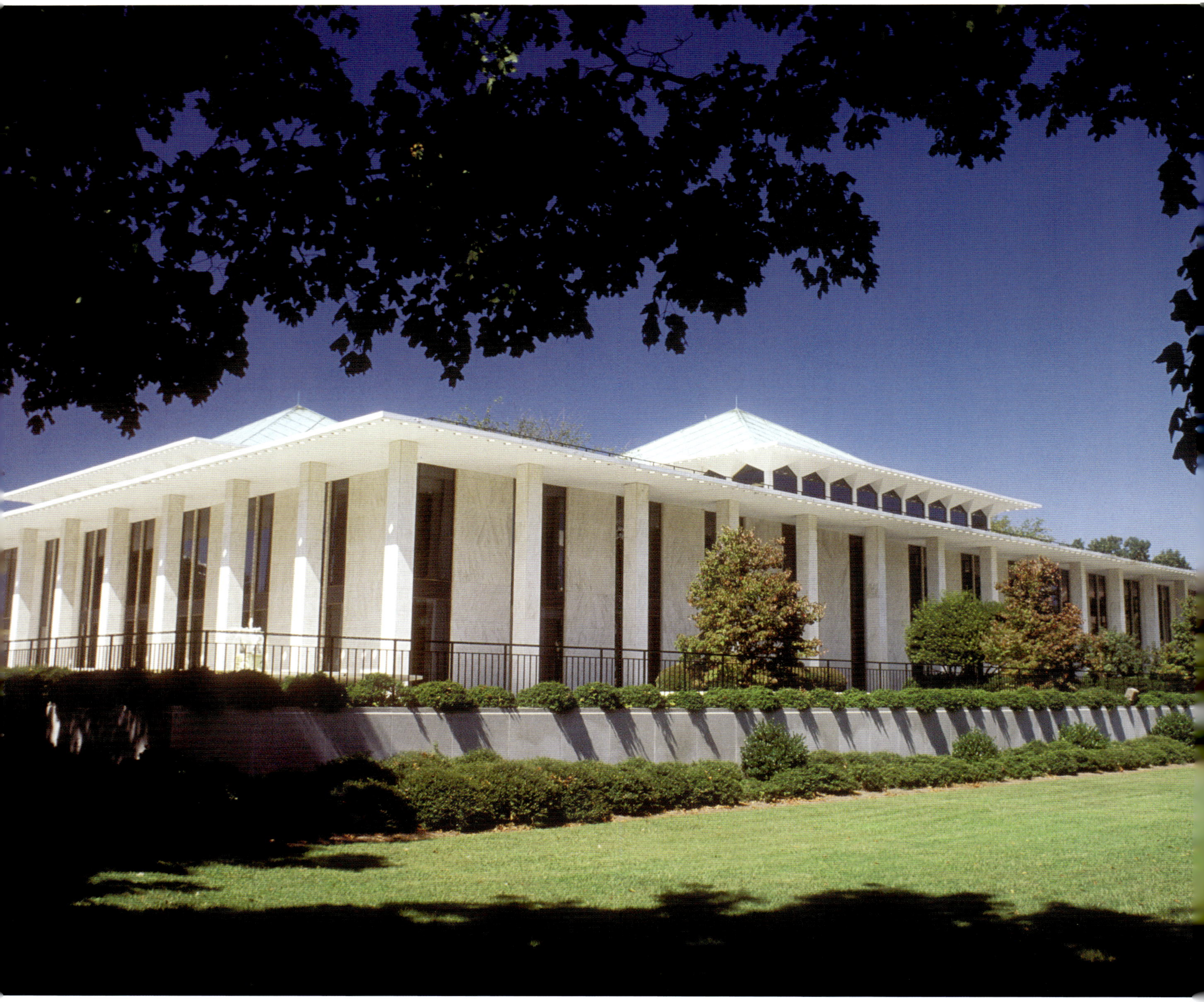

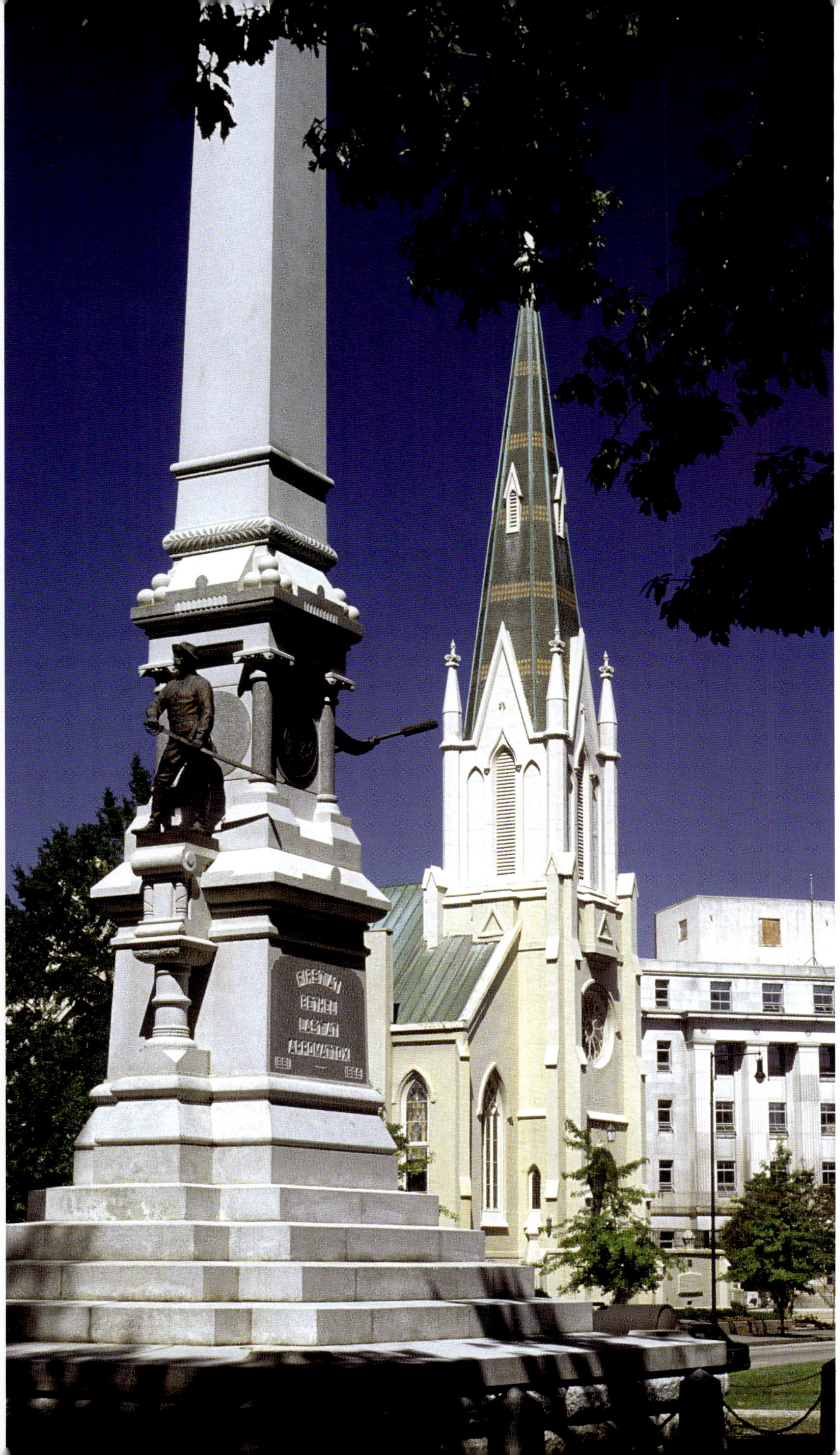

The monument at the side of the State Capitol in Raleigh is in remembrance of North Carolina's Confederate dead.

OPPOSITE PAGE: The State Legislative Building in Raleigh was completed in 1963. This majestic marble-faced structure with its series of columns sits on a 340-wide podium of North Carolina granite. Rooftop and interior gardens enhance the dramatic architecture.

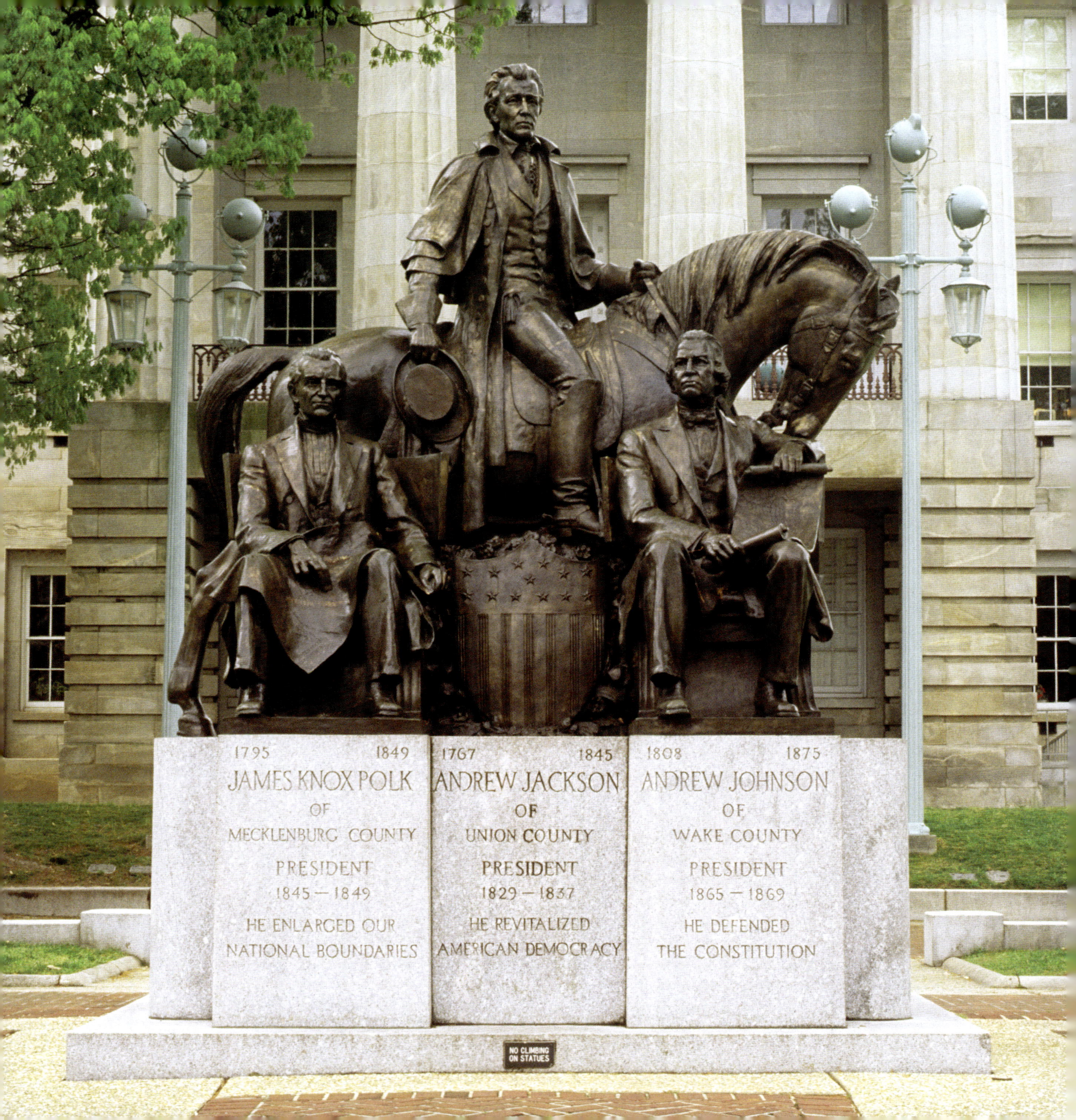
1795 1849
JAMES KNOX POLK
OF
MECKLENBURG COUNTY
PRESIDENT
1845 — 1849
HE ENLARGED OUR
NATIONAL BOUNDARIES
1767 1845
ANDREW JACKSON
OF
UNION COUNTY
PRESIDENT
1829 — 1837
HE REVITALIZED
AMERICAN DEMOCRACY
1808 1875
ANDREW JOHNSON
OF
WAKE COUNTY
PRESIDENT
1865 — 1869
HE DEFENDED
THE CONSTITUTION
NO CLIMBING
ON STATUES

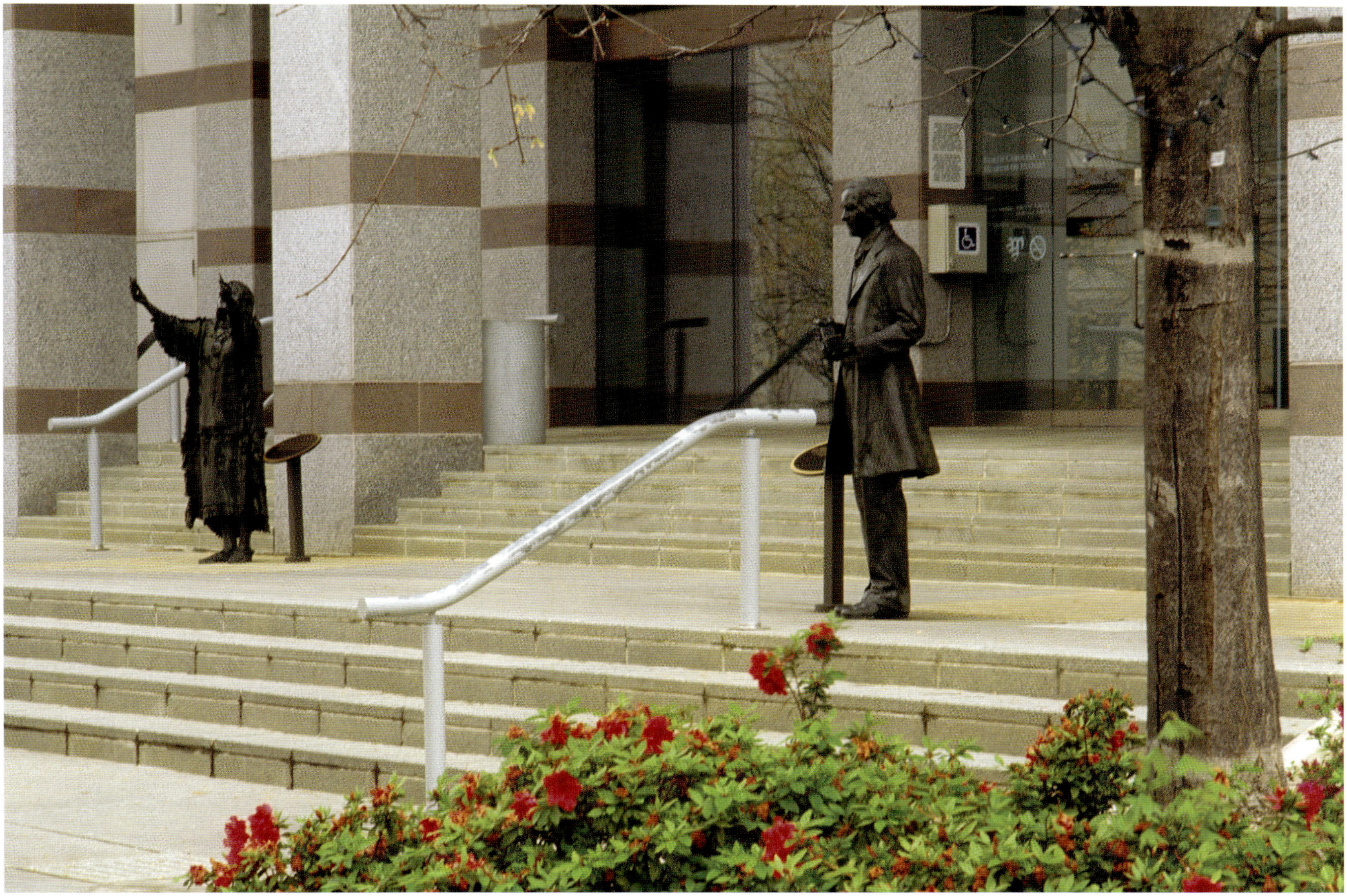

The Museum of Natural Sciences in Raleigh, known internationally as a cultural and educational center, explores the geological and biological history of the state.

OPPOSITE PAGE: Three U.S. Presidents were born in North Carolina: James K. Polk, Andrew Jackson and Andrew Johnson. This imposing bronze memorial is situated by the State Capitol Building in Raleigh.

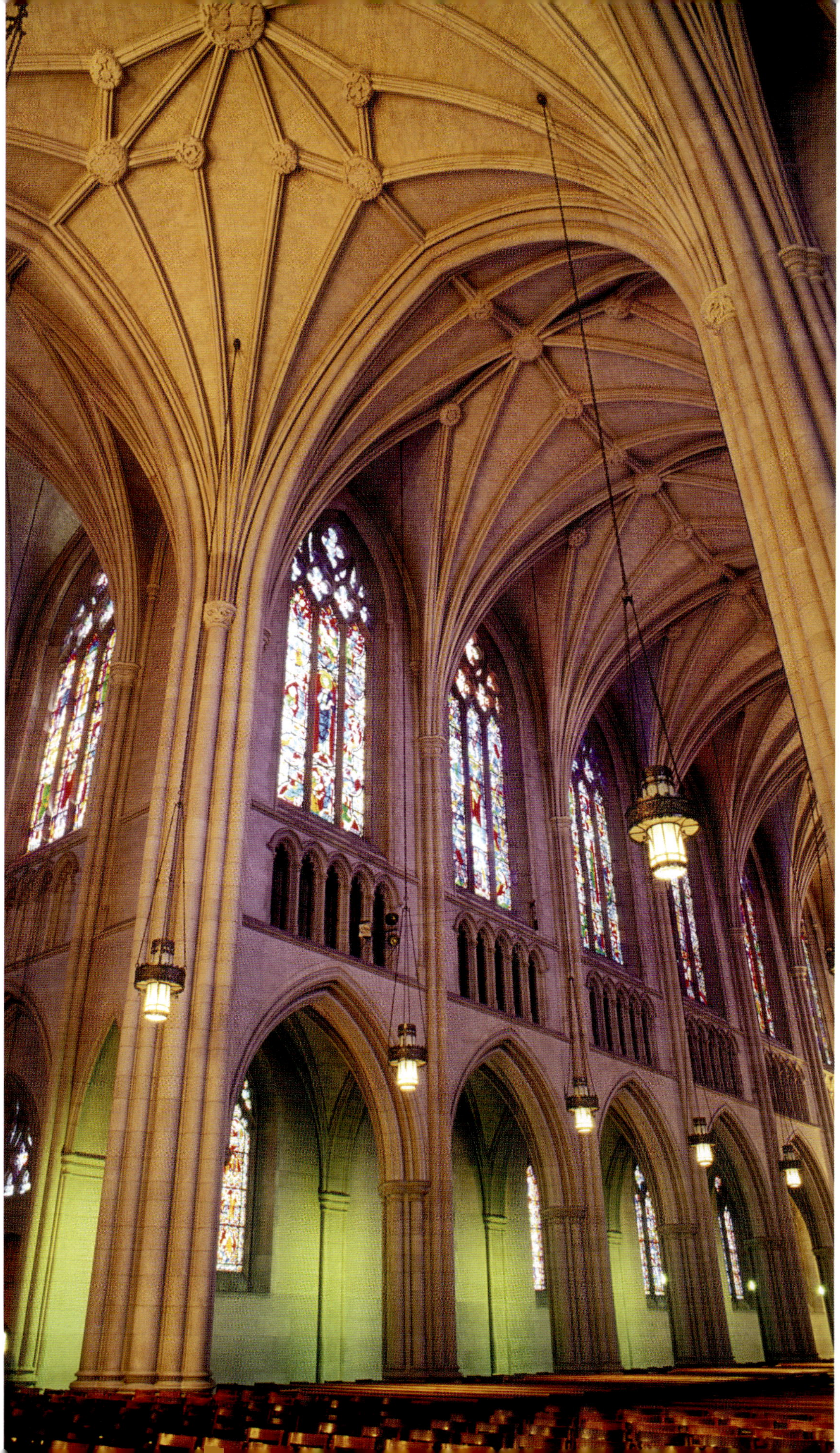

Located on the university's highest ridge, the magnificent neo-Gothic Duke University Chapel in Durham is characterized by its ribbed vaults, pointed arches and massive stone piers. The tower (opposite) contains a 50-bell carillon. In addition to its architecture, the university is well known for academics, research and athletics.

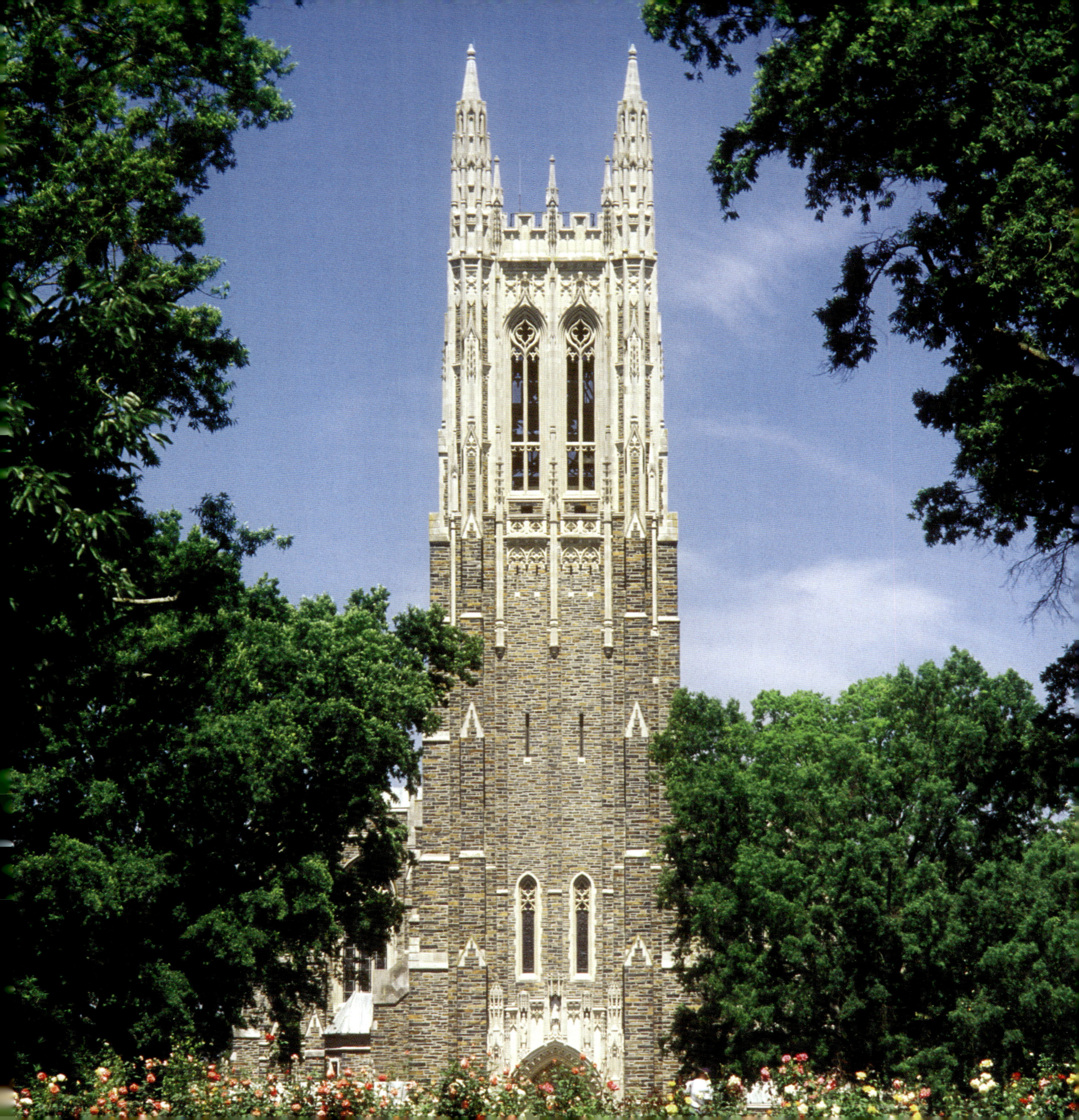

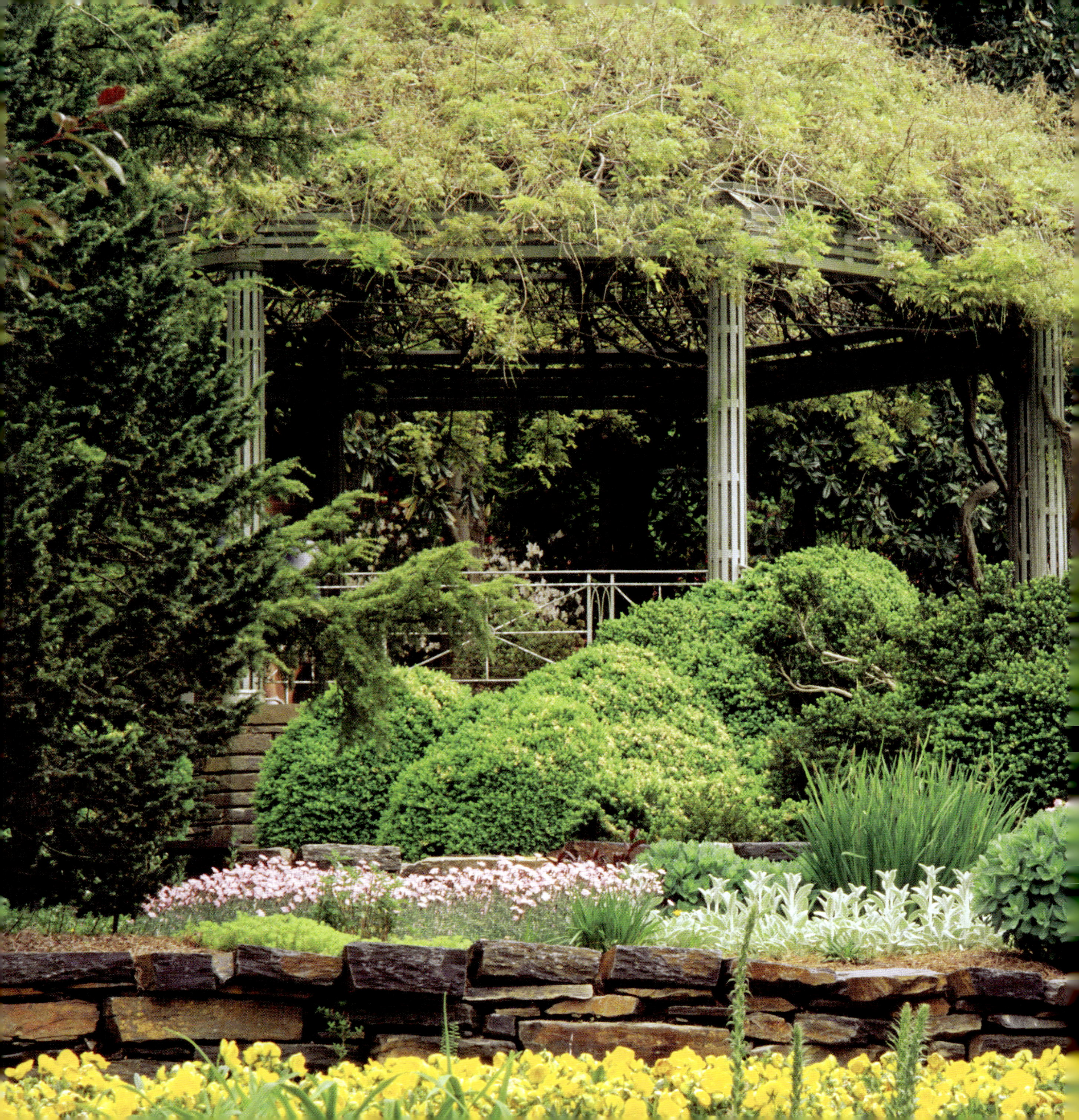

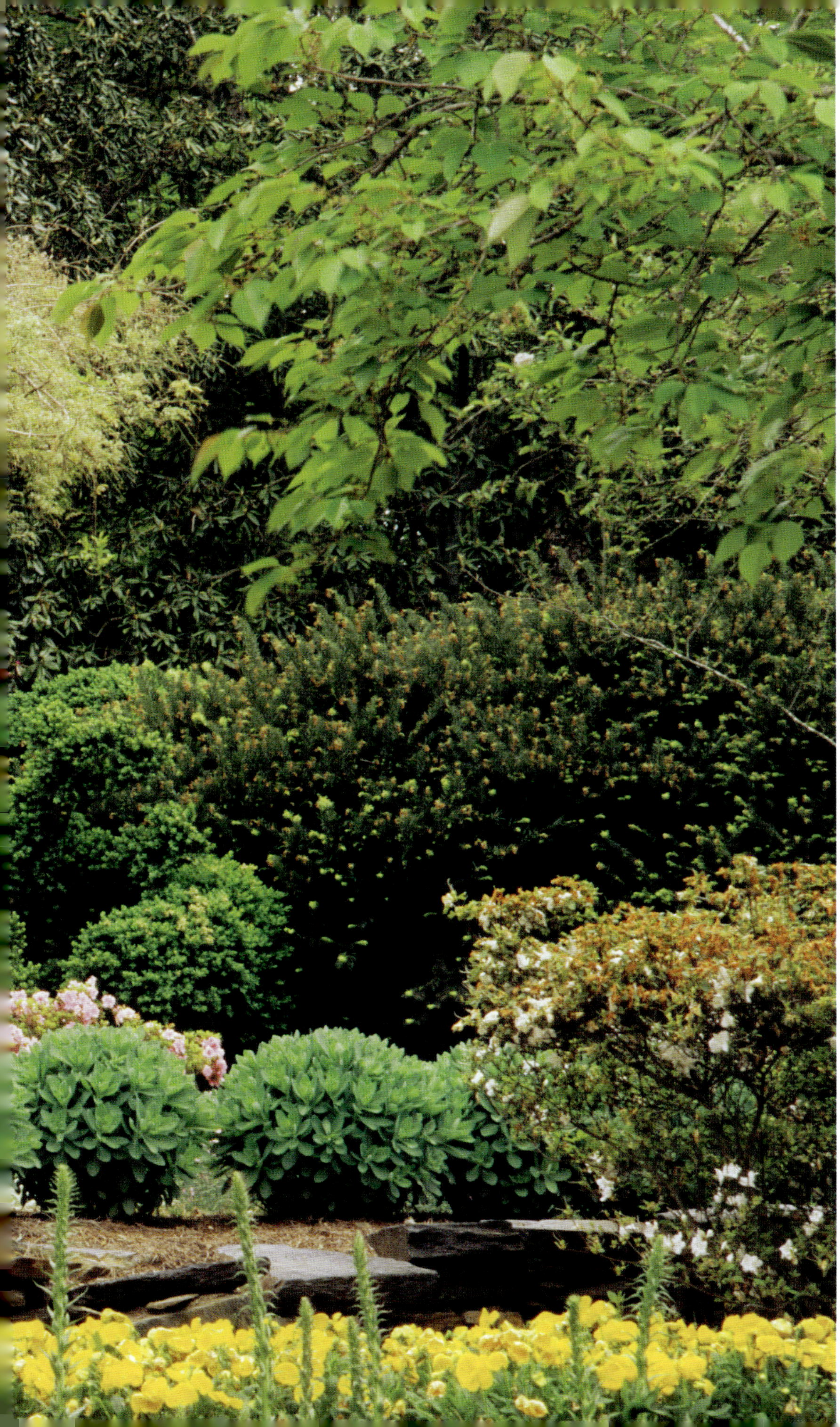

The Sarah P. Duke Gardens in Durham is often referred to as the crown jewel of Duke University. It is regarded as one of the finest public gardens in the country.

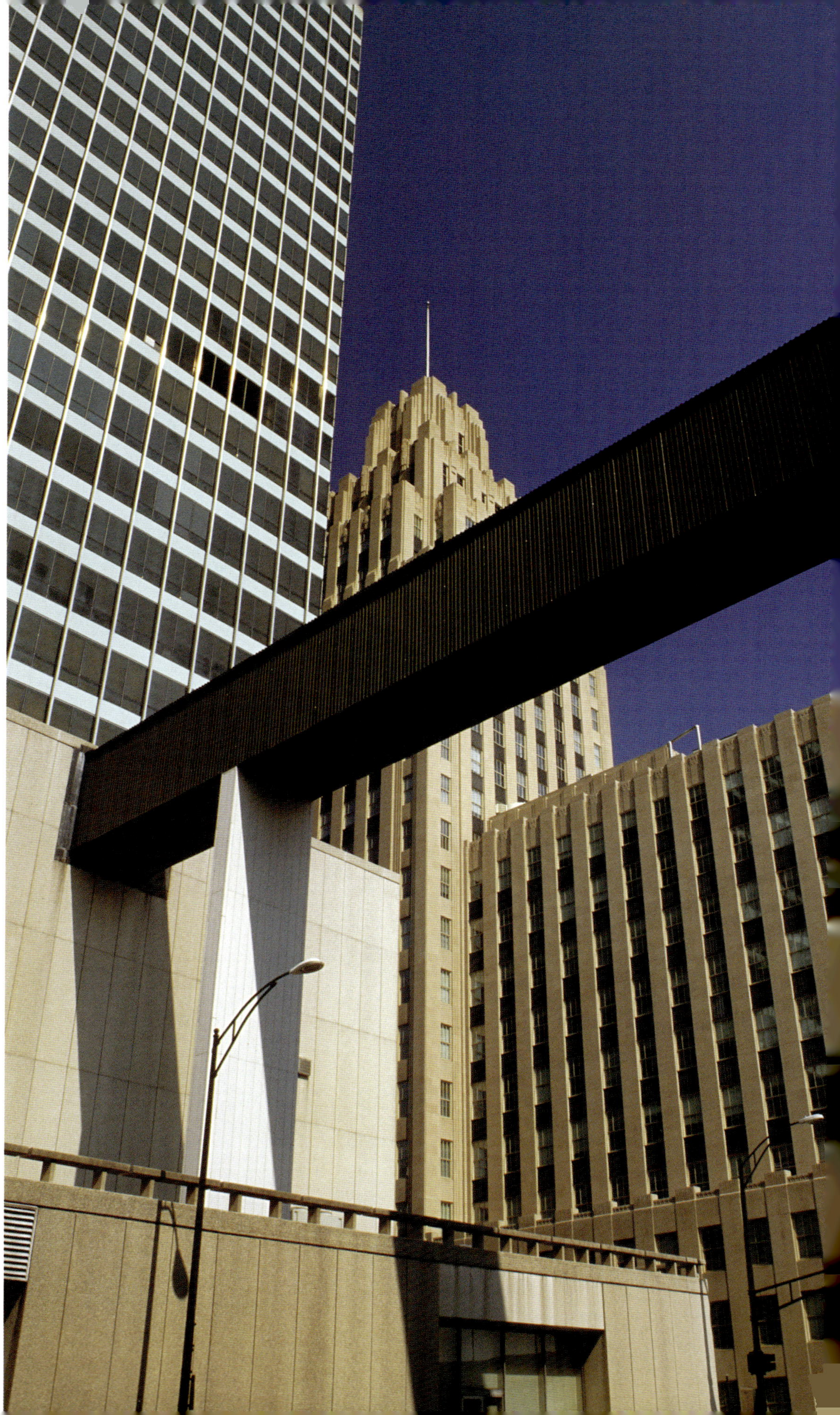

In contrast to historic Old Salem, the skyscrapers of Winston-Salem present an imposing view of life today. A pedestrian walkway makes life more convenient for office workers. Winston and nearby Salem consolidated in 1913, establishing the two cities as a successful textile and tobacco center.

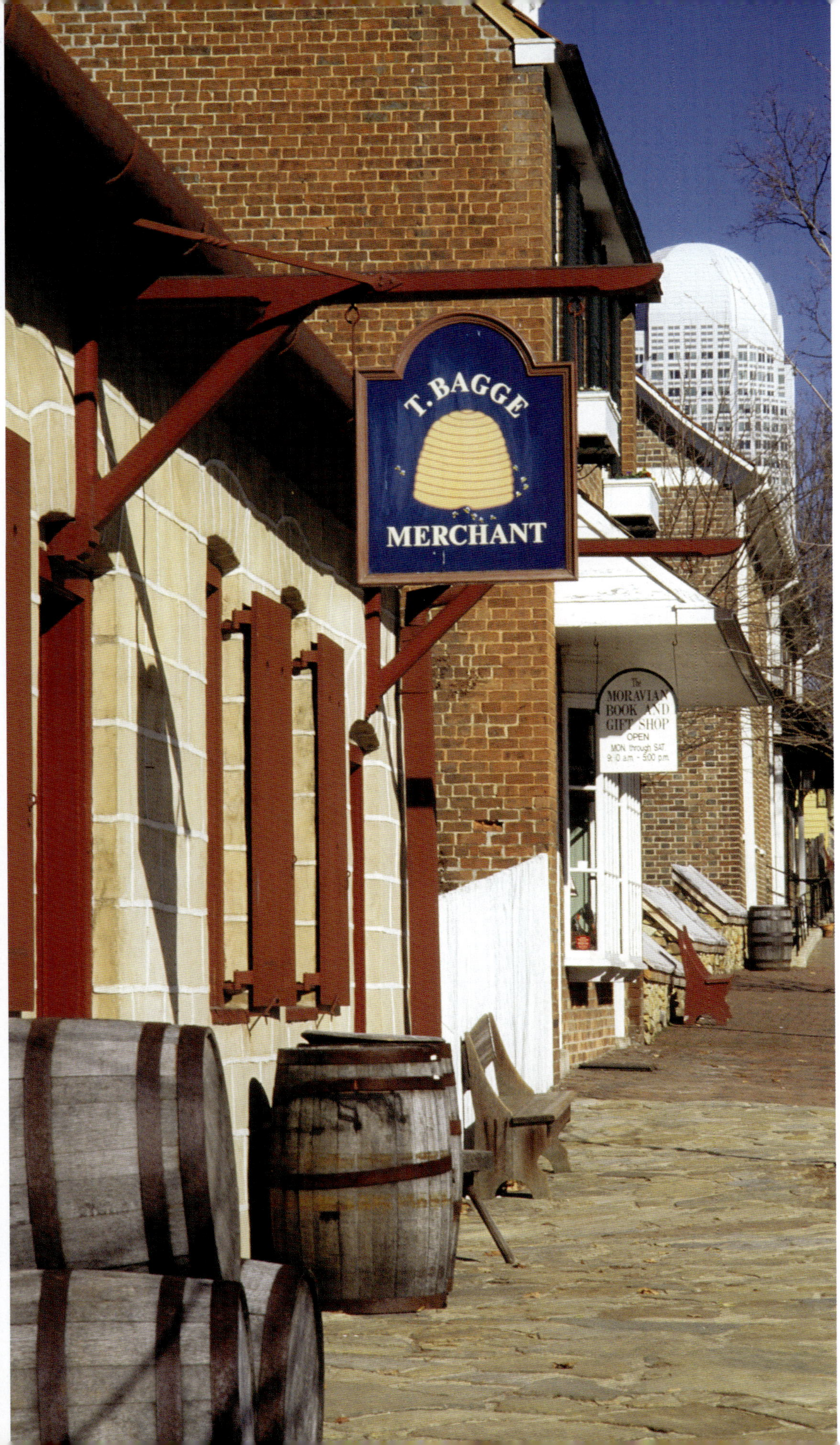

Visitors relive history as they stroll along the cobbled streets of Old Salem, one of the leading attractions of North Carolina. Costumed hosts provide a tour of this restored Moravian community of the early South with its old-world charm and crafts.

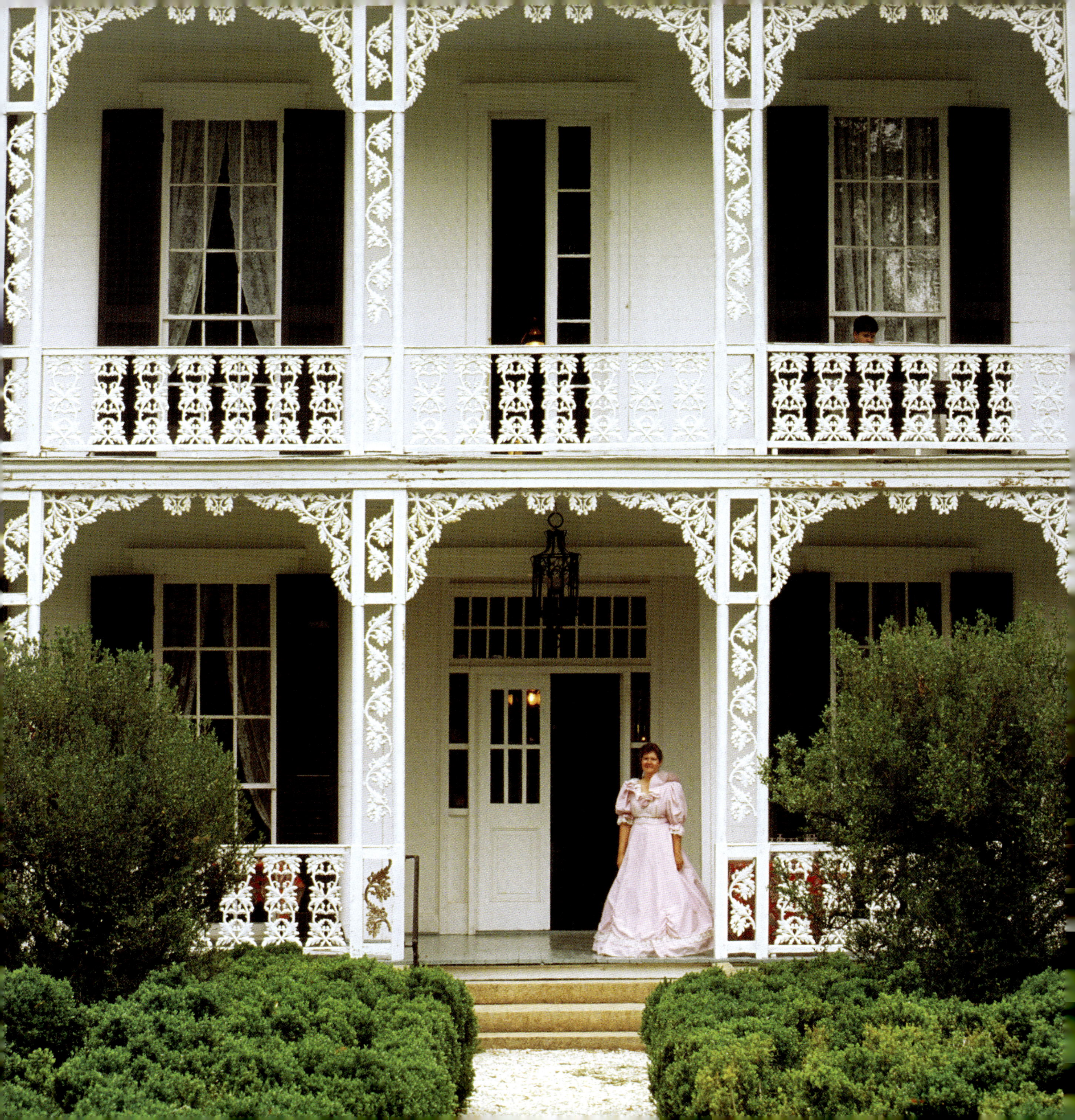

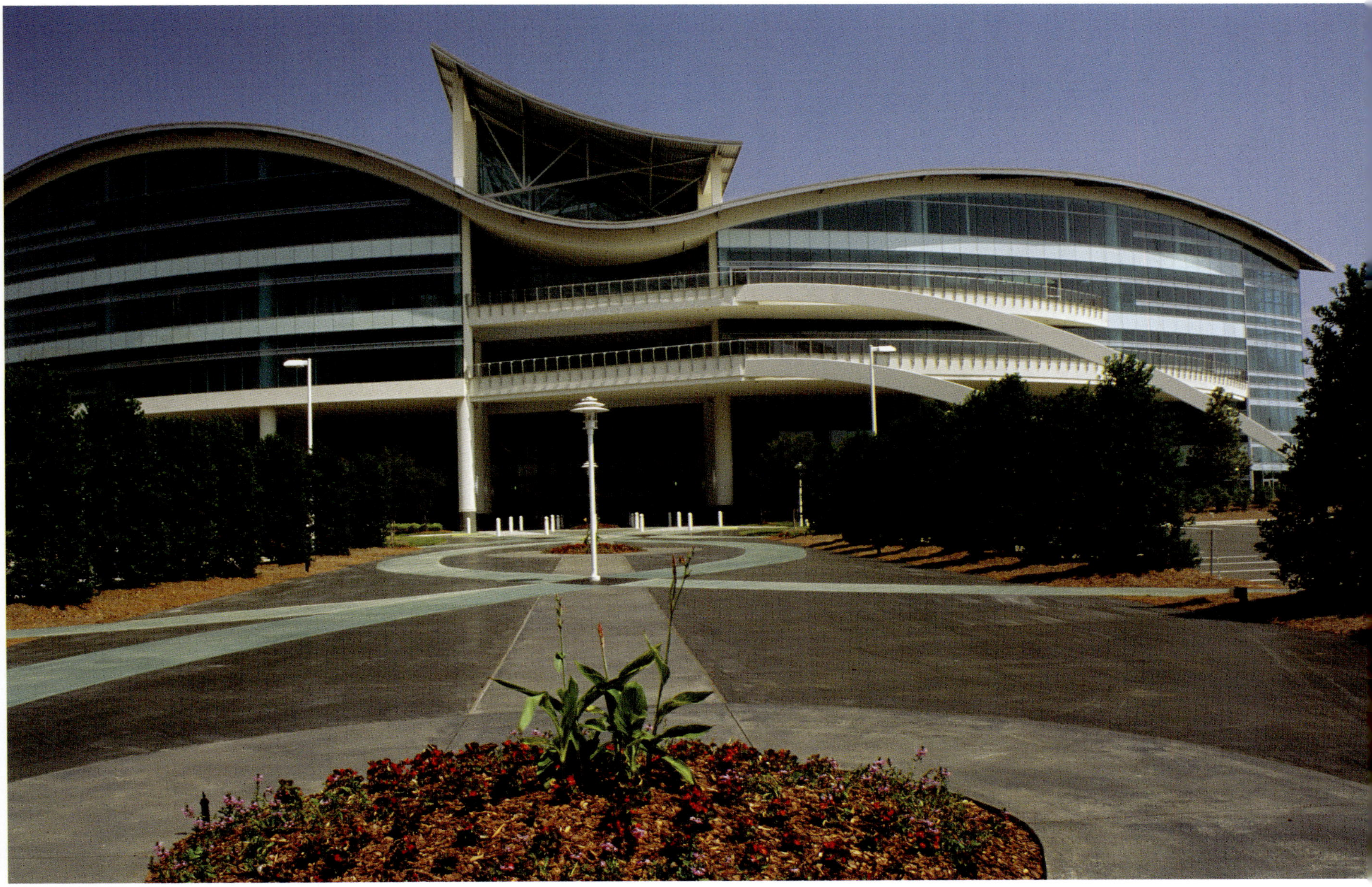

The city of High Point is generally known as the furniture capital of the world. The Showplace building is a venue for the High Point Market, the largest furnishing industry trade show anywhere.

OPPOSITE PAGE: The city of Salisbury was founded in 1753 and quickly became a prosperous trading center. It also had one of the largest prison camps maintained by the Confederate Army. Still prominent in the historic district is the Dr. Josephus Hall House, built in 1820 as the Salisbury Female Academy and later purchased by the surgeon of the Confederate prison.

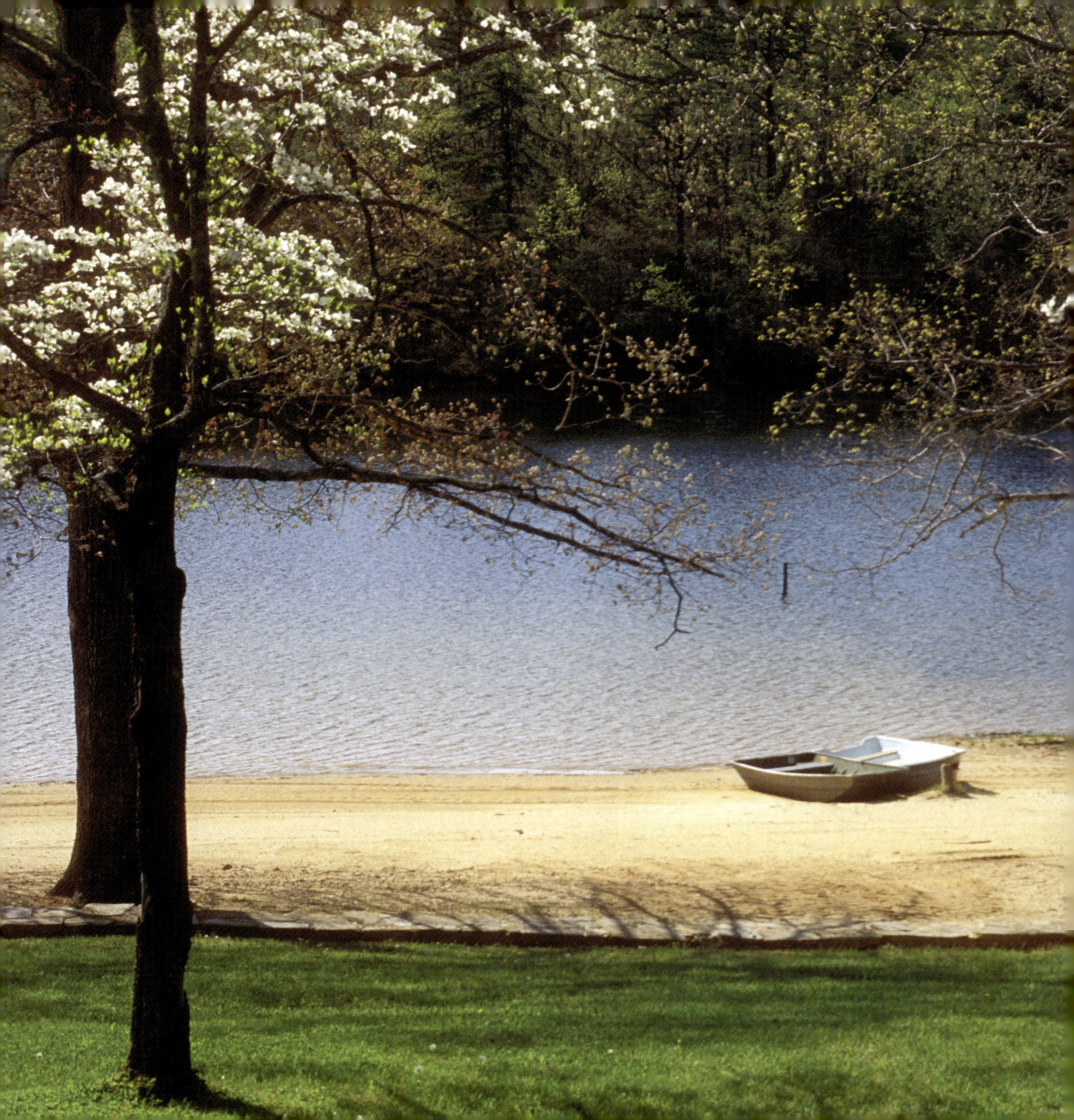

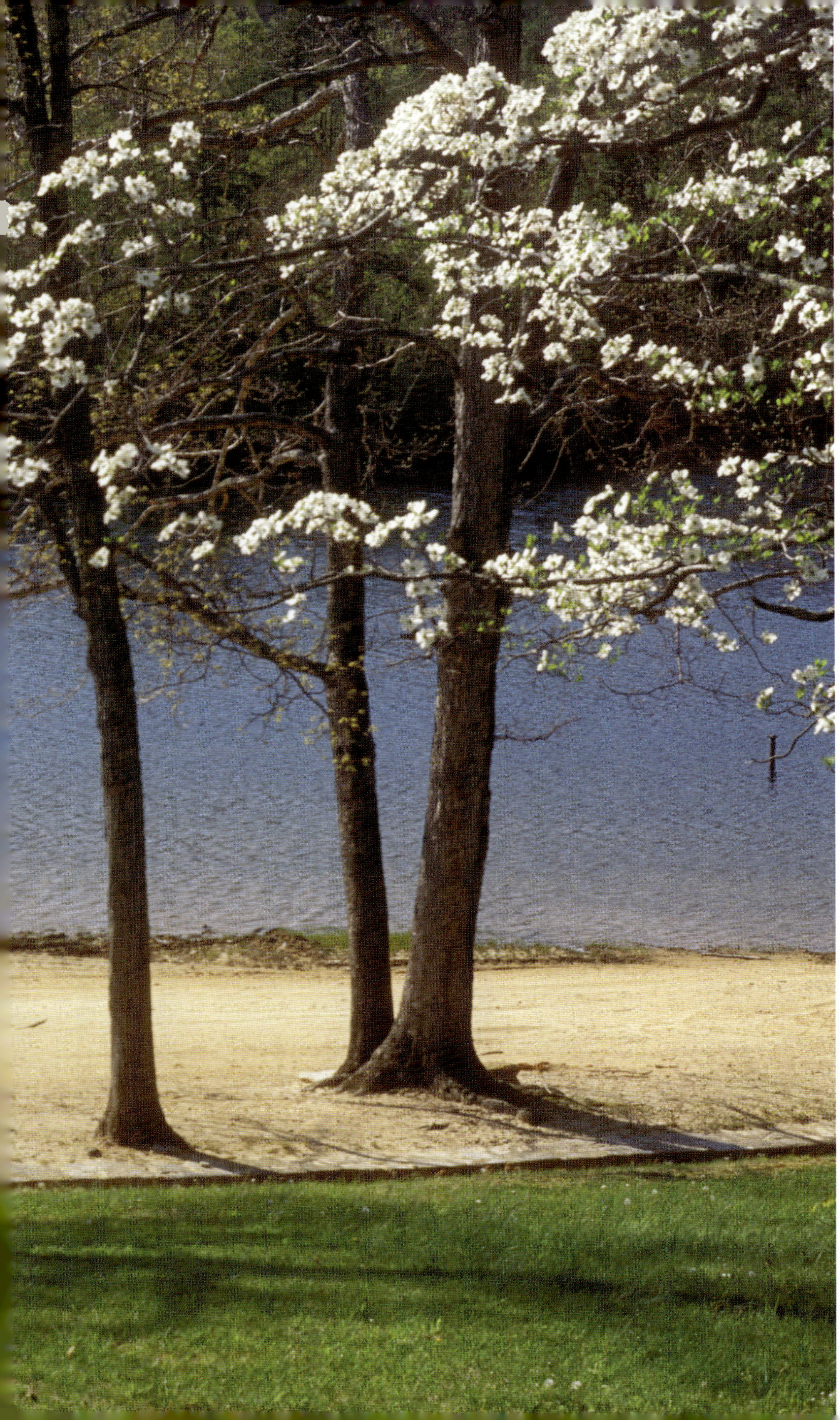

There are many small lakes in the state parks, ideal for a gentle boat ride. In the spring, dogwood trees explode into bloom. The state has no fewer than 34 state parks, 14 national parks and four national forests, each with its own spectacular scenery.

FOLLOWING PAGE: These pristine sand dunes are on Bodie Island near Oregon Inlet. They are part of the Outer Banks, which provides a barrier of low, sandy islands. Tides and storms continue to move the dunes in an ever-shifting landscape.

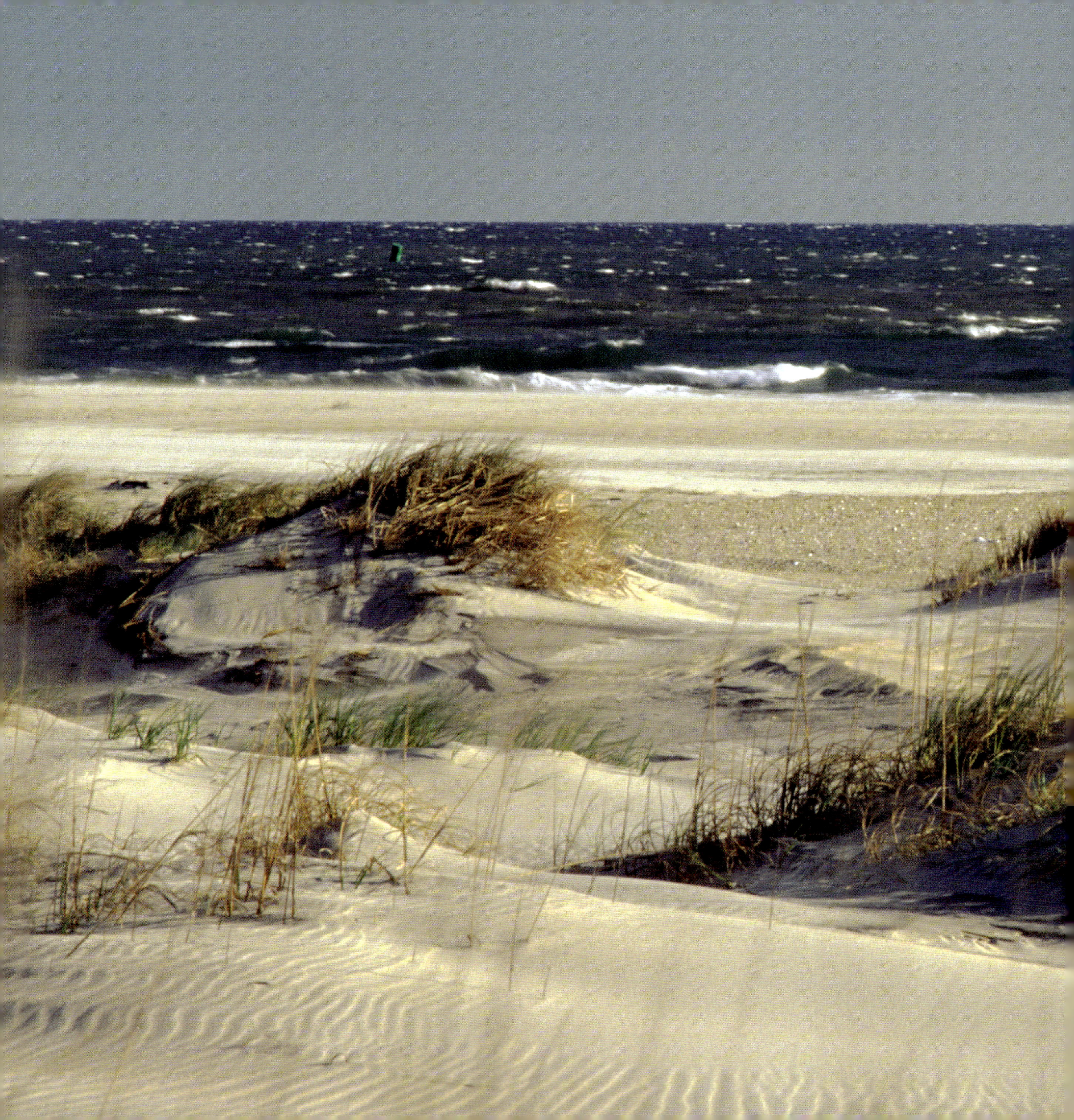

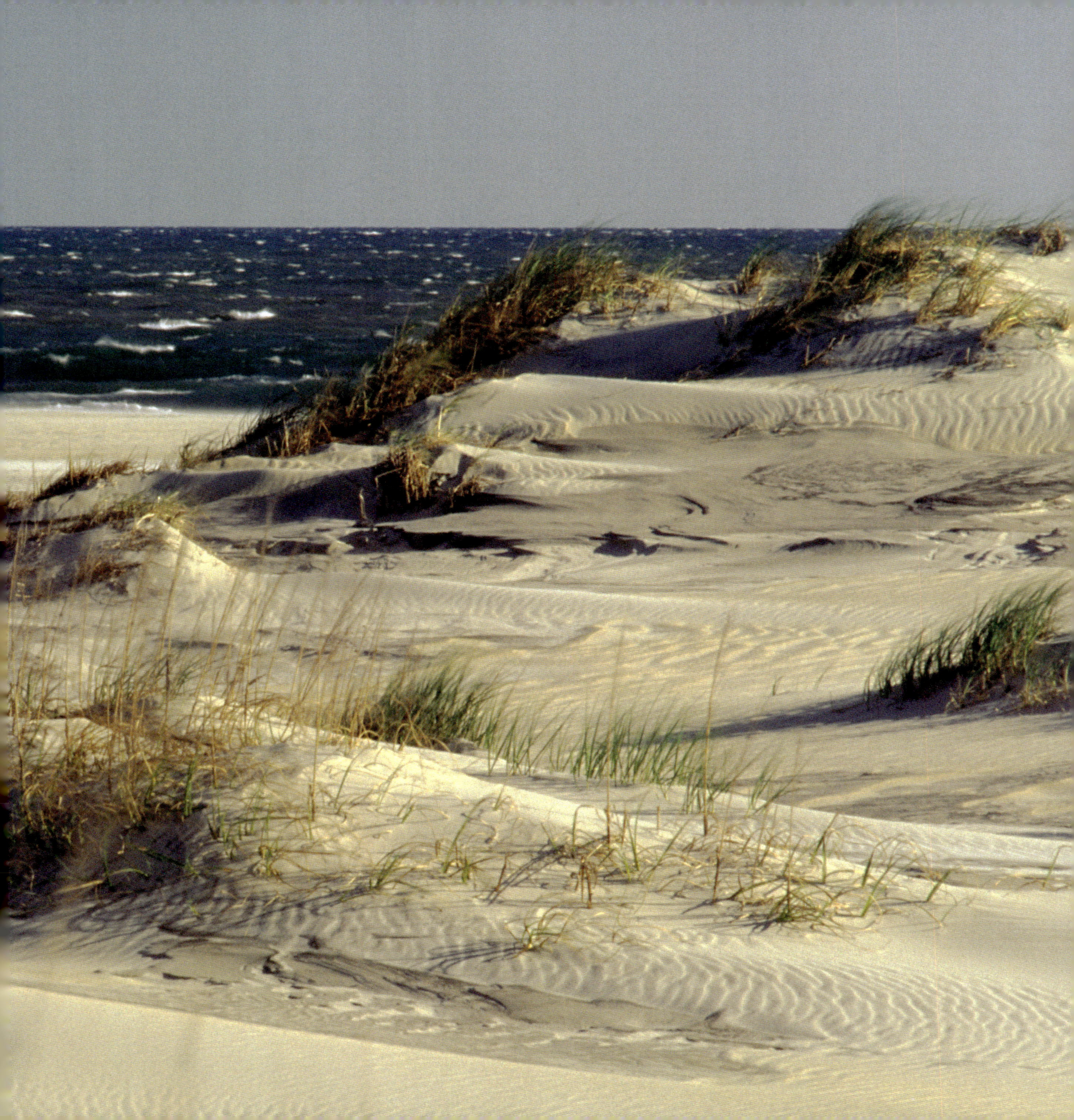

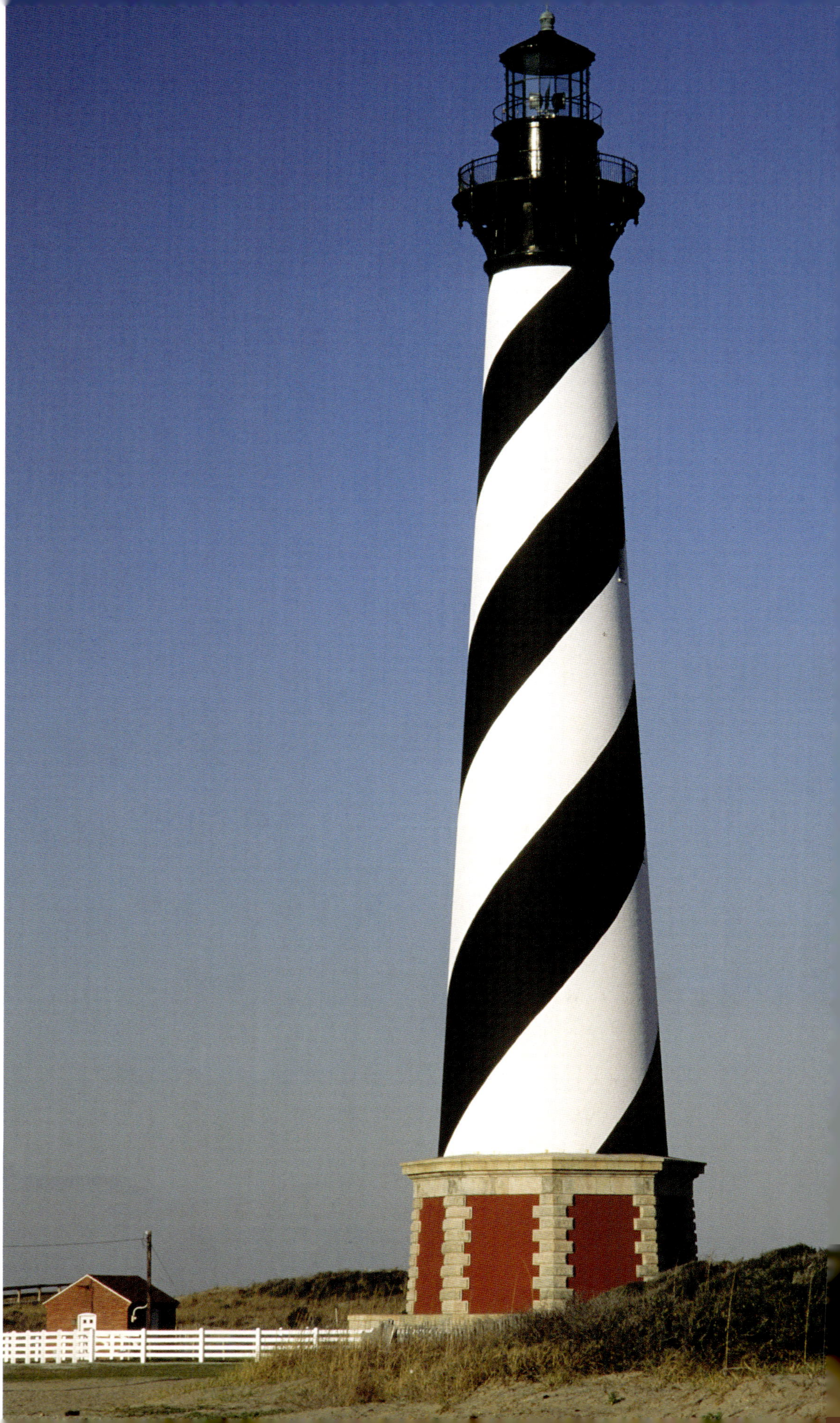

At 208 feet, the Cape Hatteras Lighthouse is the tallest brick lighthouse in the United States. Built in 1870, it has warned ships away from the treacherous Diamond Shoals, also known for decades as the Graveyard of the Atlantic.

OPPOSITE PAGE: The reconstructed 16th-century sailing vessel *Elizabeth II* is a composite representation of the ship *Elizabeth*, one of the ships that sailed in the 1585 expedition to the New World.

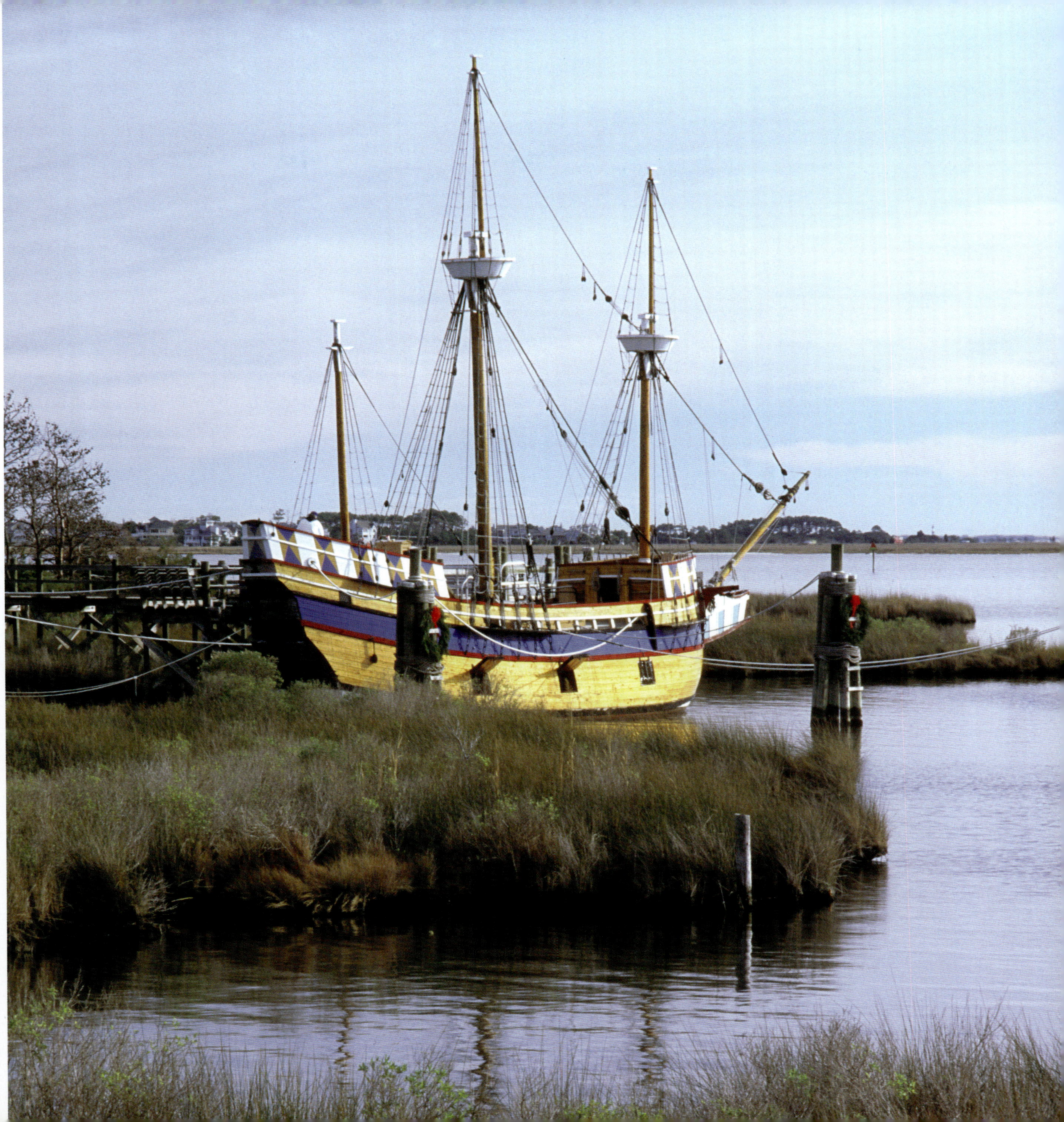

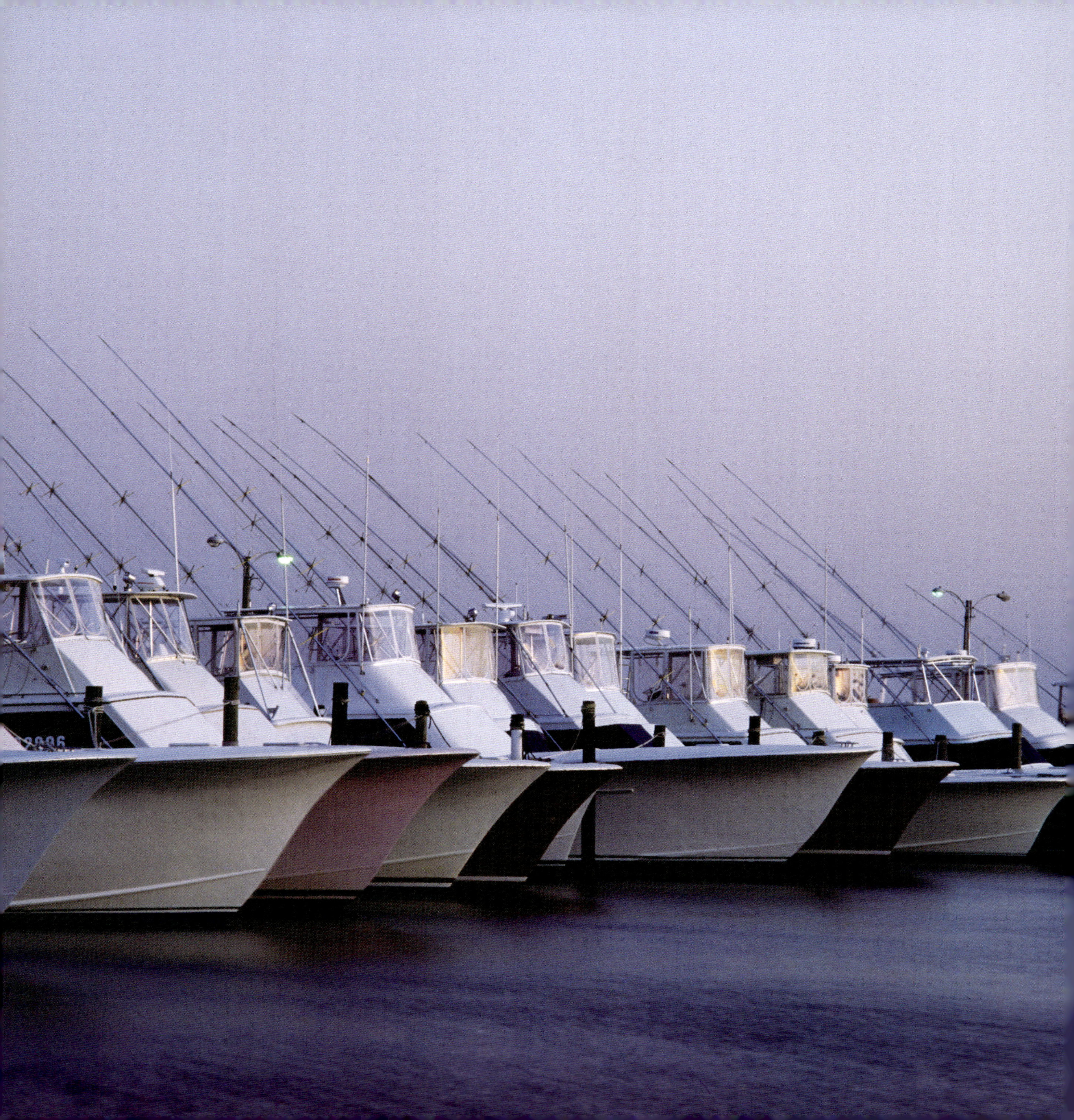

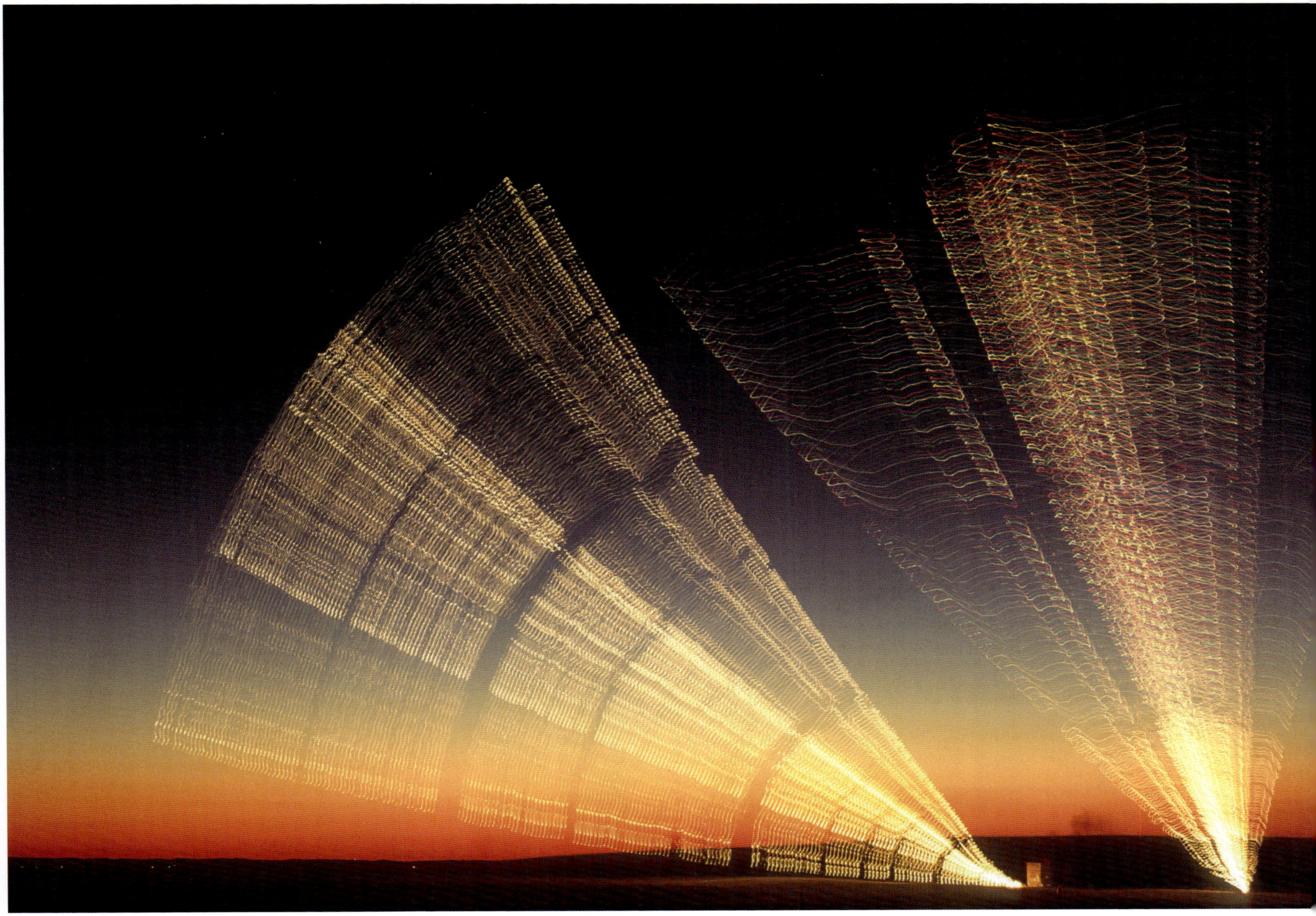

The Kites with Lights is an annual event on Bodie Island in the Outer Banks. It takes place at Jockey's Ridge, the highest active sand dune on the Atlantic Coast with a height of over 100 feet.

OPPOSITE PAGE: A purple dusk colors deep-sea fishing boats in the Oregon Inlet on the Outer Banks. As the northernmost inlet in North Carolina, it is an important passageway for commercial and recreational fishing boats.

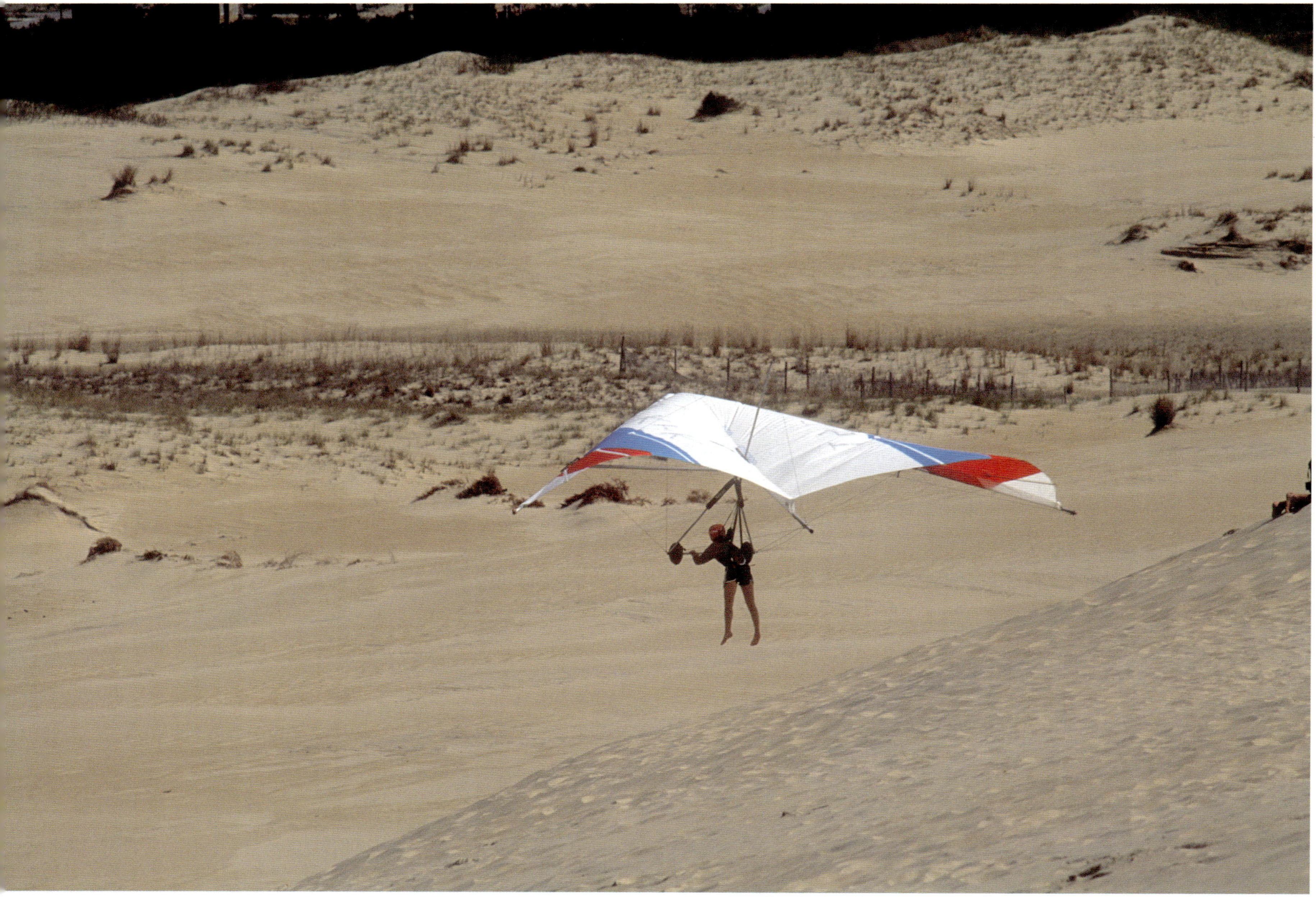

Hang gliders enjoy the dramatic scenery of the dunes on Bodie Island.

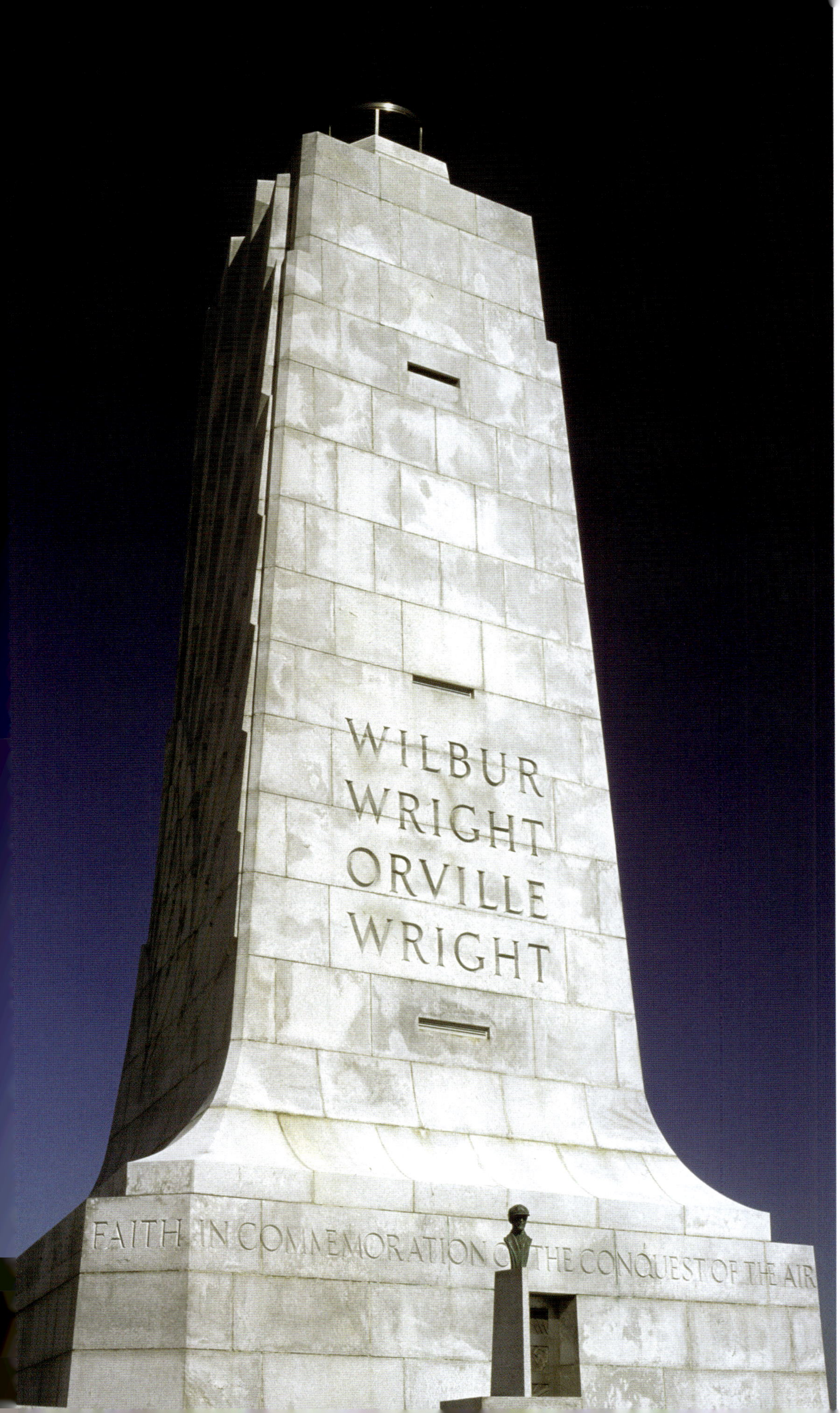

The Wright Brothers National Memorial commemorates an event that changed the world forever. On December 17, 1903, the first heavier-than-air machine left the ground by its own power at Kitty Hawk on the Outer Banks of North Carolina. The rest is aviation history, and it is owed to the two unassuming brothers, Wilbur and Orville Wright.

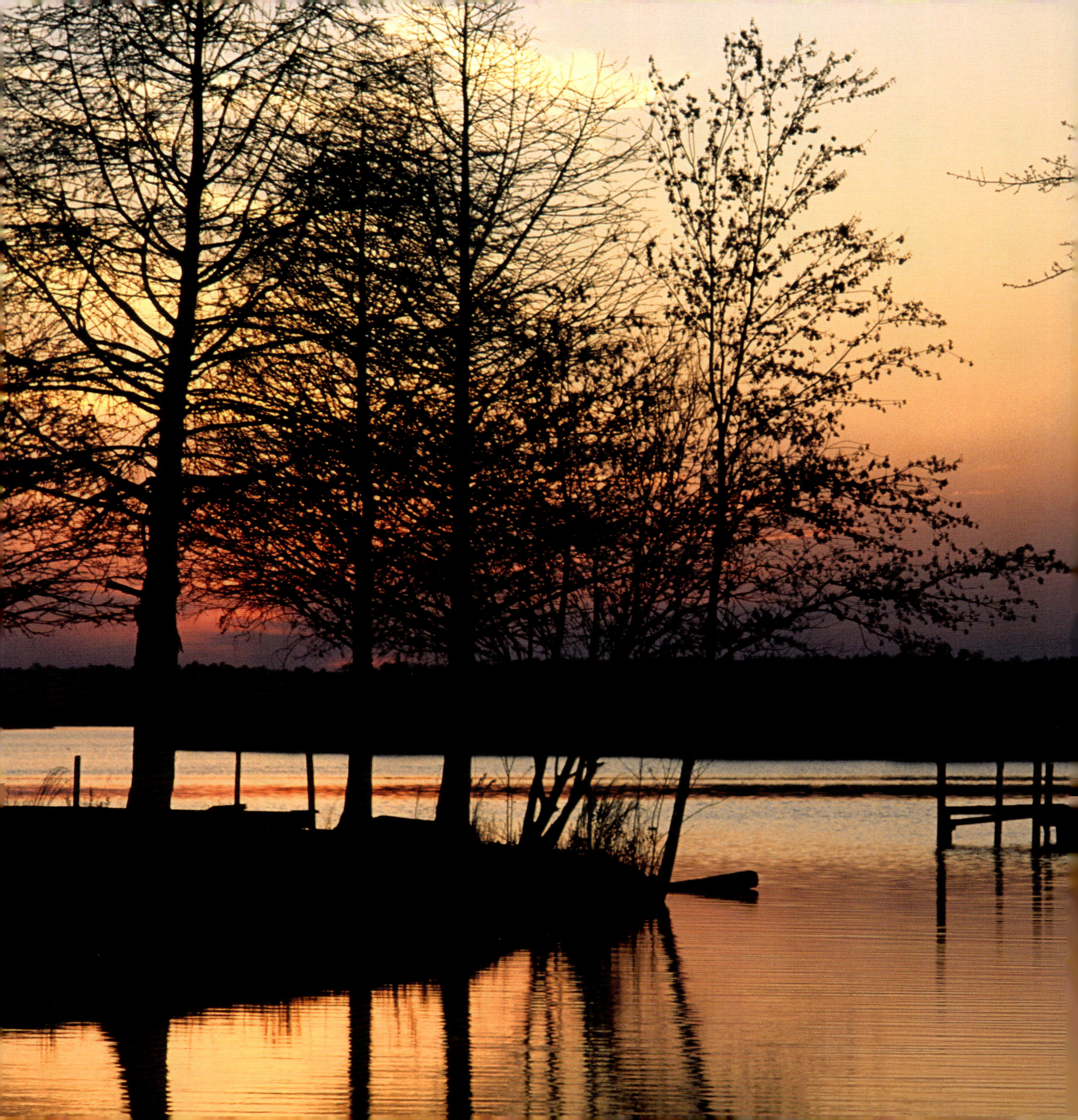

Brought by the Spaniards in the 1500s, wild horses still graze on the salt marsh on the Outer Banks, protected by the North Carolina National Estuarine Research Reserve. The area was established to preserve the fragile natural areas and wildlife.

OPPOSITE PAGE: The setting sun is reflected in the coastal marshes in the Pungo River area. The area is famous for its seafood, the blue crab being one specialty of the region.

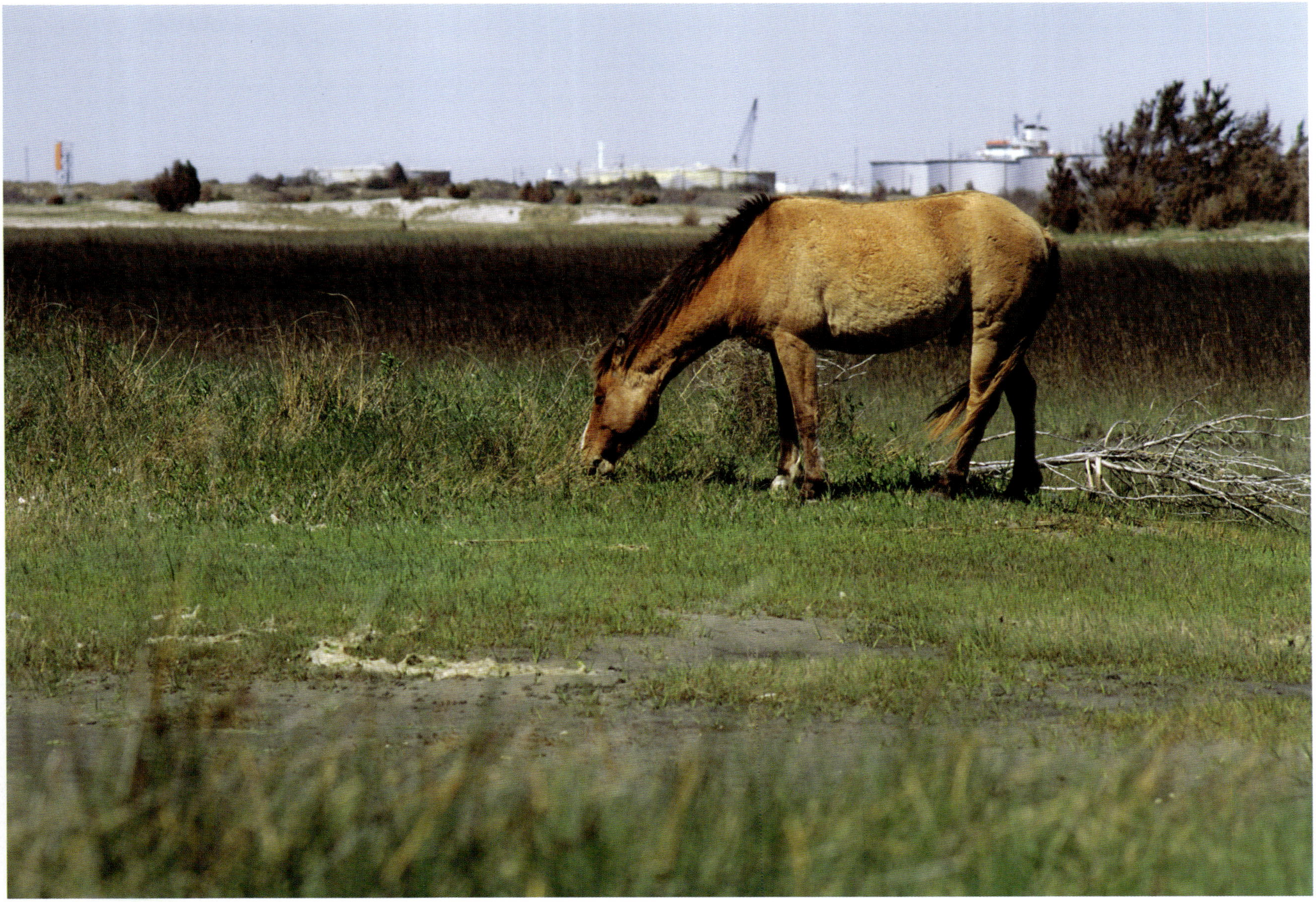

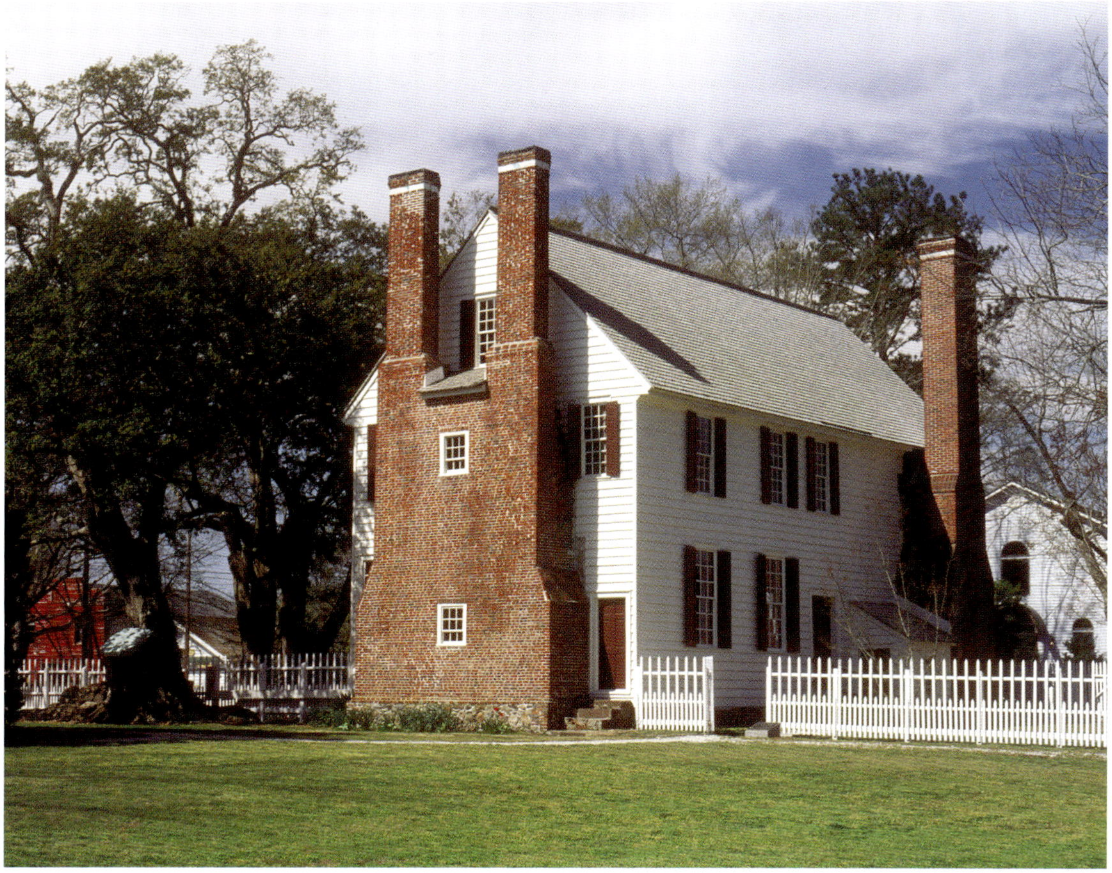

Situated in the Bath Historic District in the central coast region, the Palmer-Marsh House was built in 1751. One of its most remarkable features is its 17-foot-wide double chimney.

OPPOSITE PAGE: Tryon Palace in the New Bern Historic District commands attention in its Georgian splendor. Built between 1767 and 1770, it is the site of North Carolina's first permanent capitol. George Washington is said to have danced there.

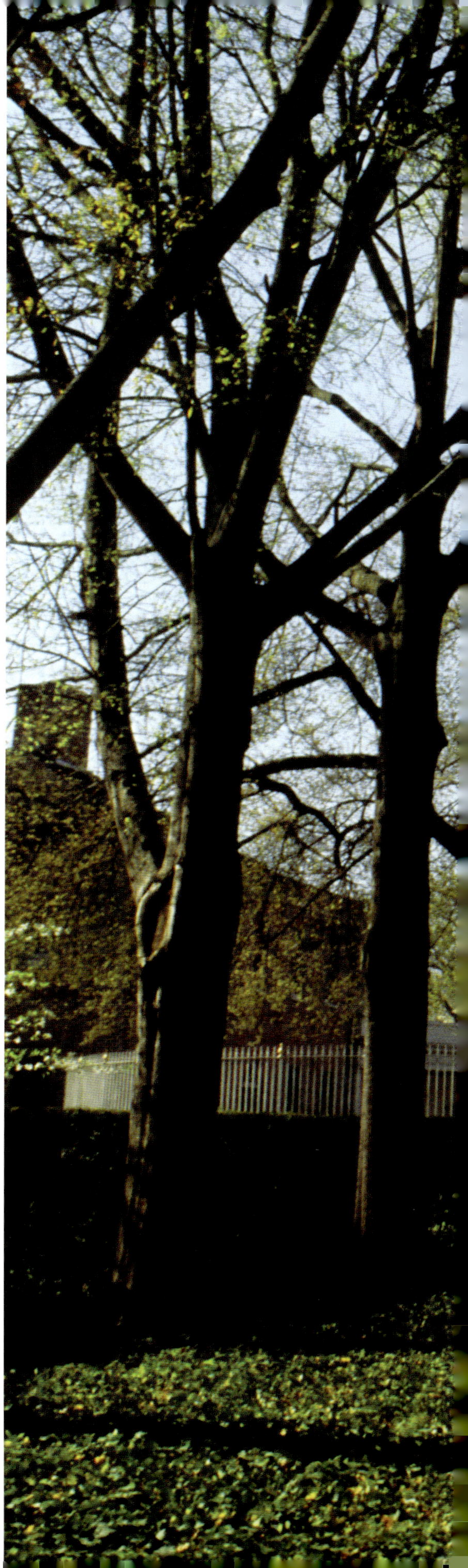

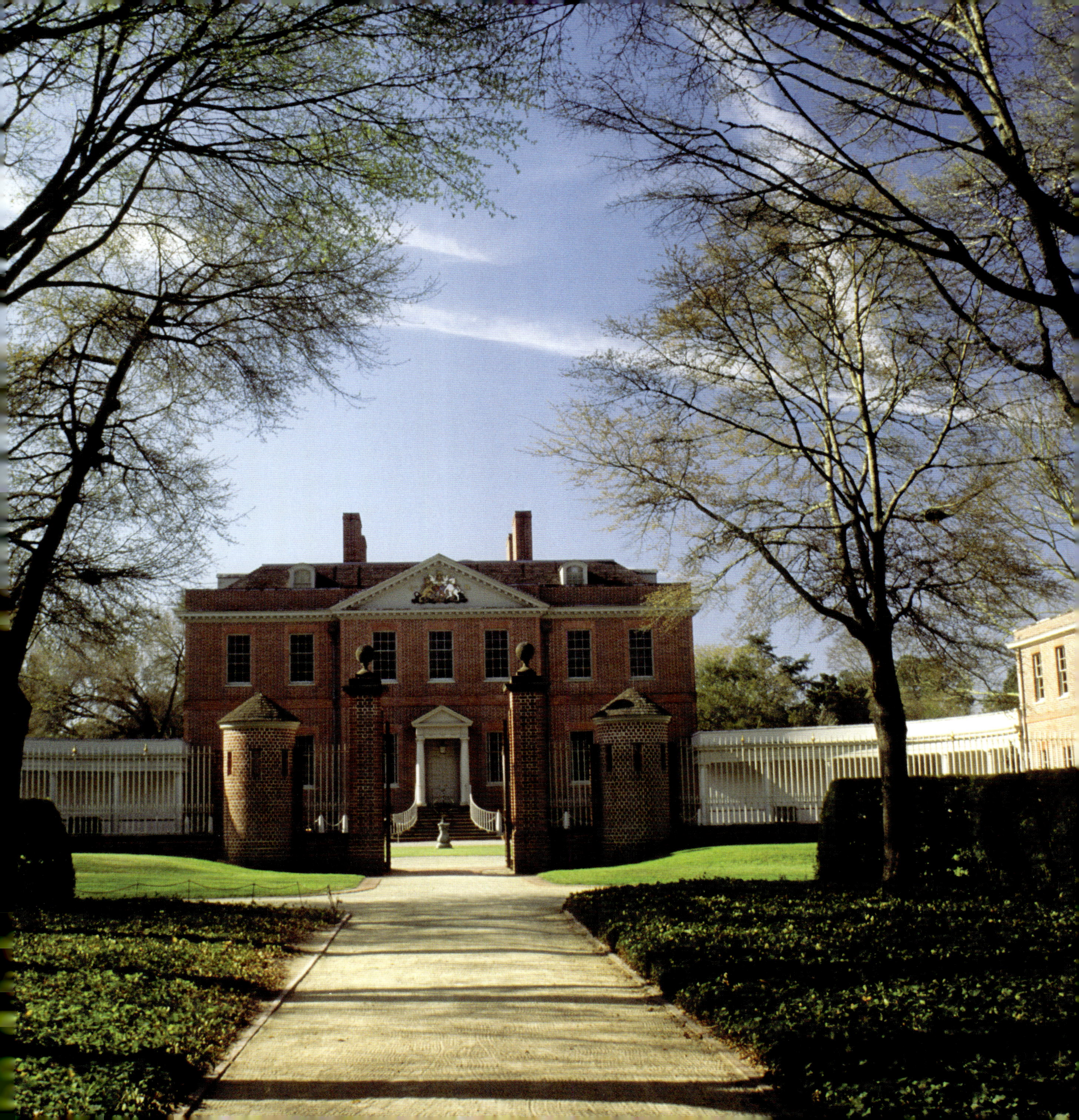

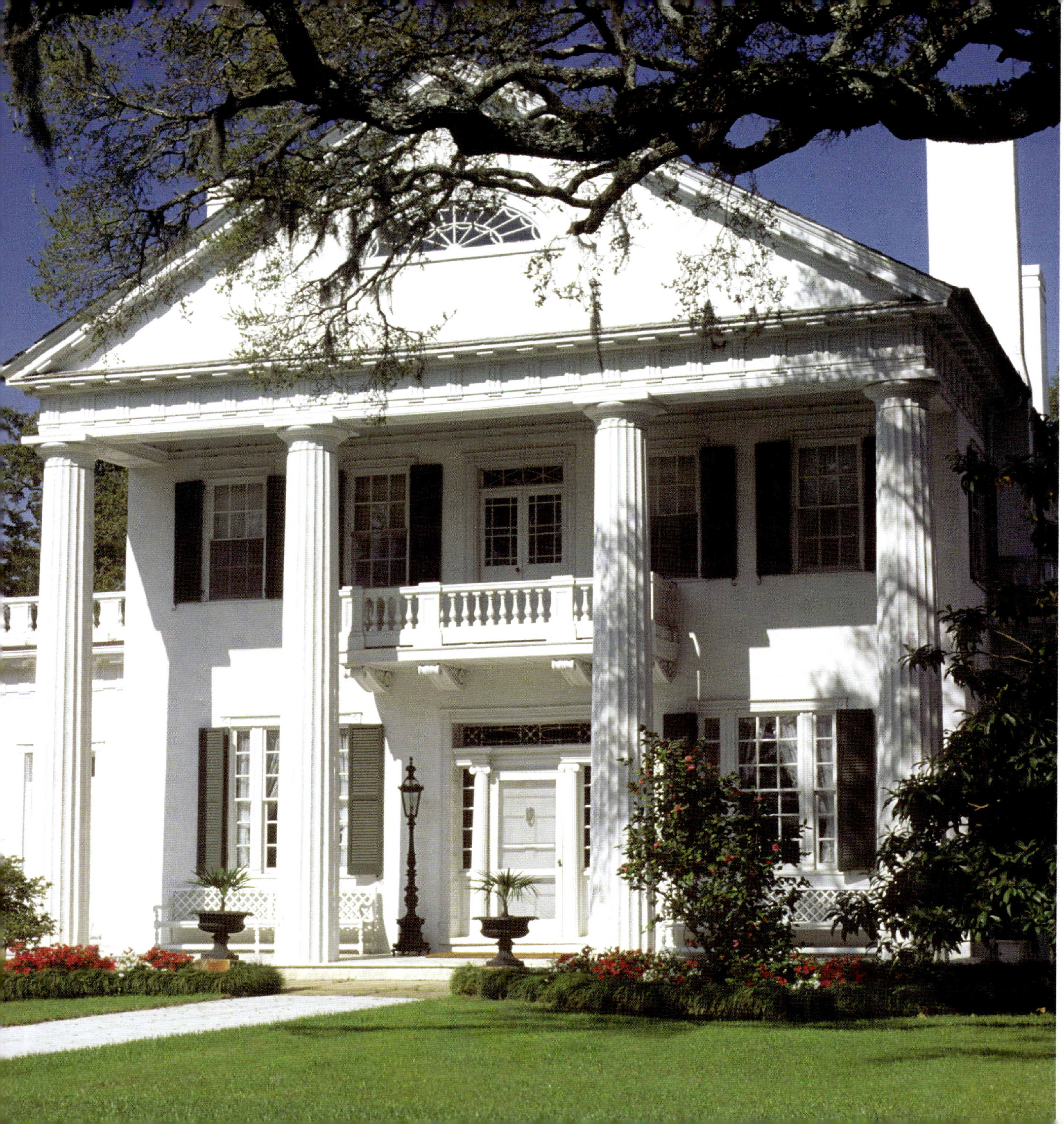

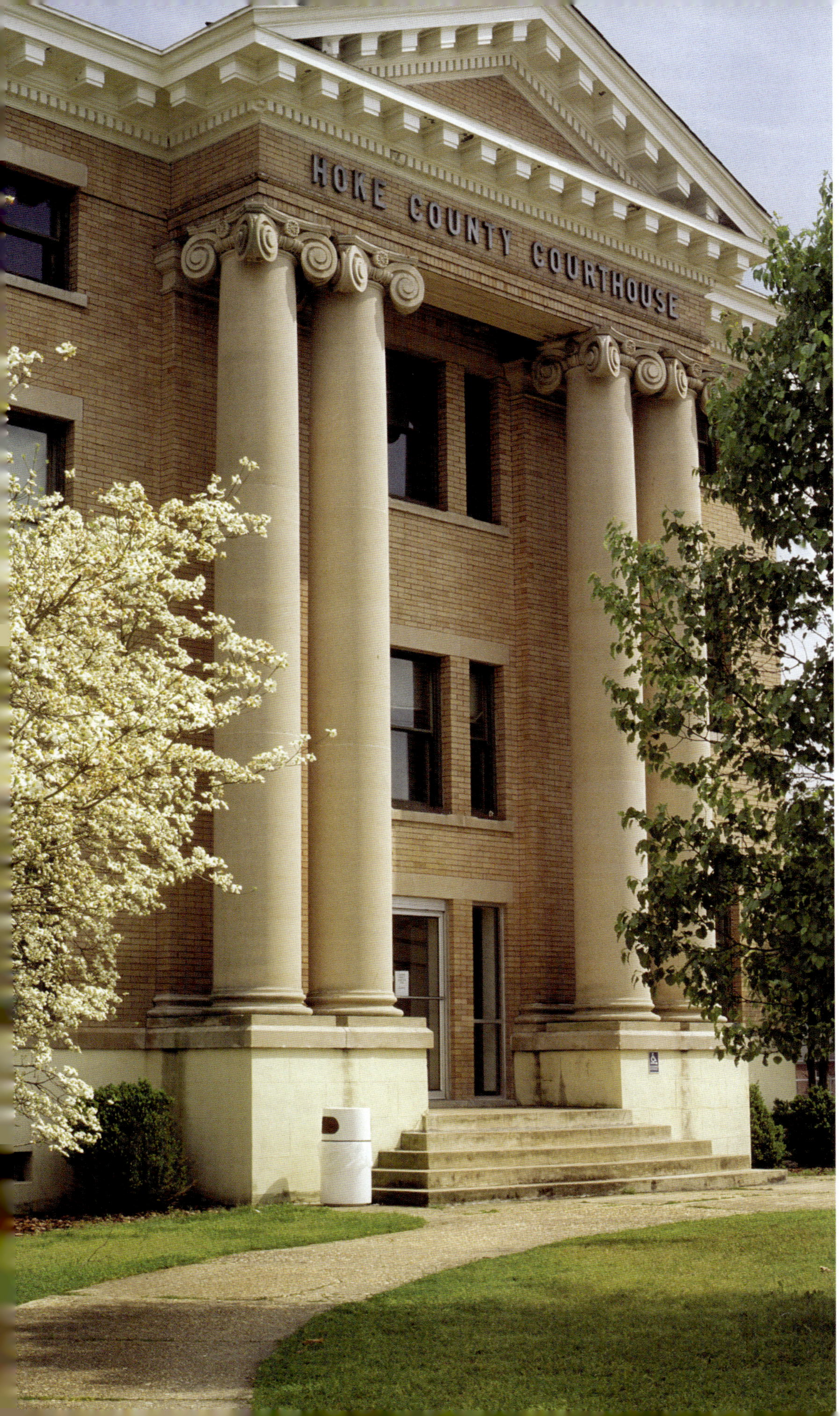

The Orton Plantation house, dating from 1735, is a remarkable example of antebellum architecture. Flowering fruit trees, camellias, and a profusion of spring and summer annuals have made it a favorite destination for visiting gardeners. Walking trails offer views of the Cape Fear River.

OPPOSITE PAGE: The grand columnar entrance of the Hoke County Courthouse in the south coast region presents an imposing center for justice. Designed in the classical revival style, it is in the National Register of Historic Places.

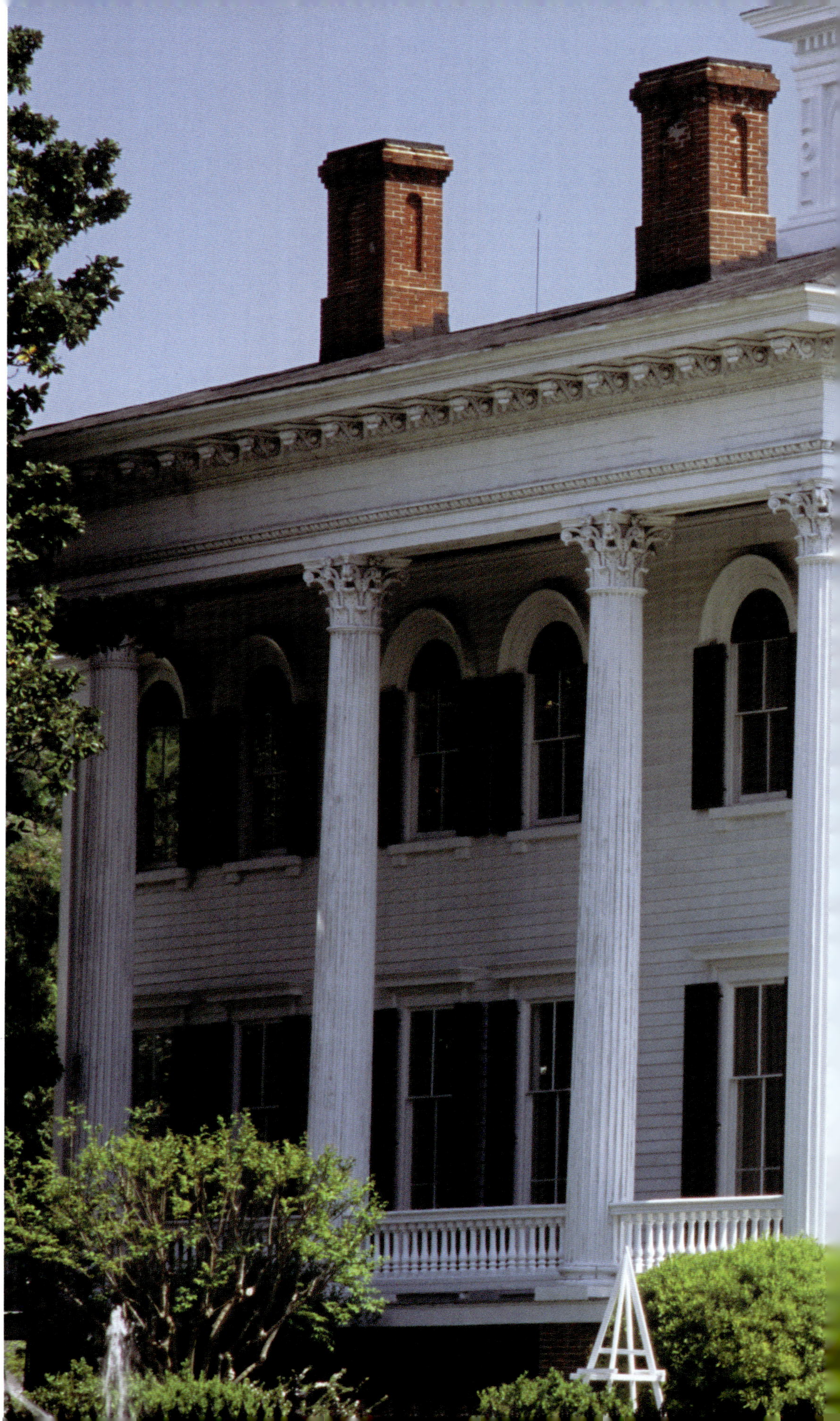

The Bellamy Mansion Museum of History and Design Arts is located in the heart of the Wilmington Historic District. Built just before the Civil War, it is one of North Carolina's premier examples of antebellum architecture – a mixture of Greek Revival and Italianate styles.

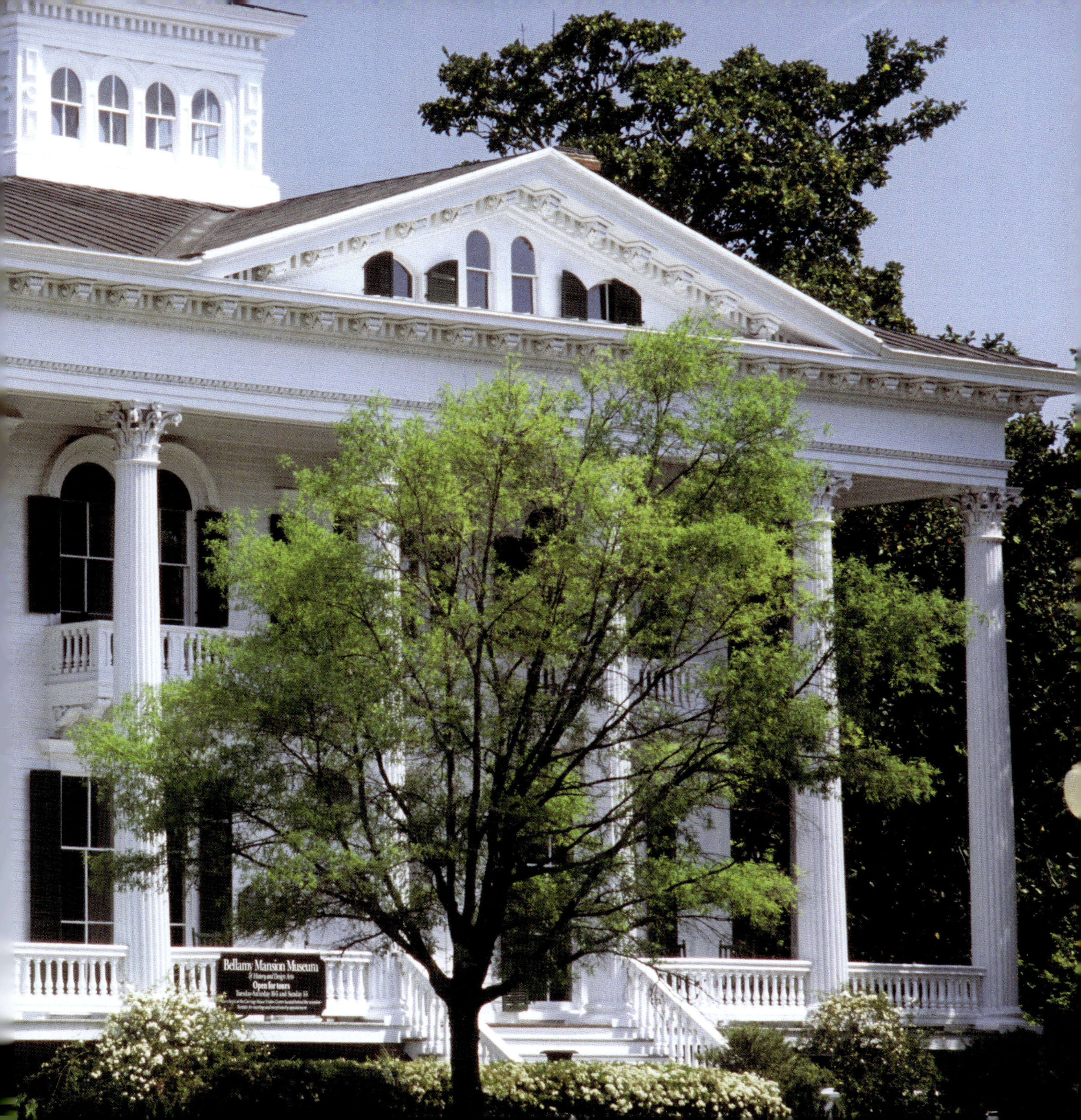
Bellamy Mansion Museum
Open for tours

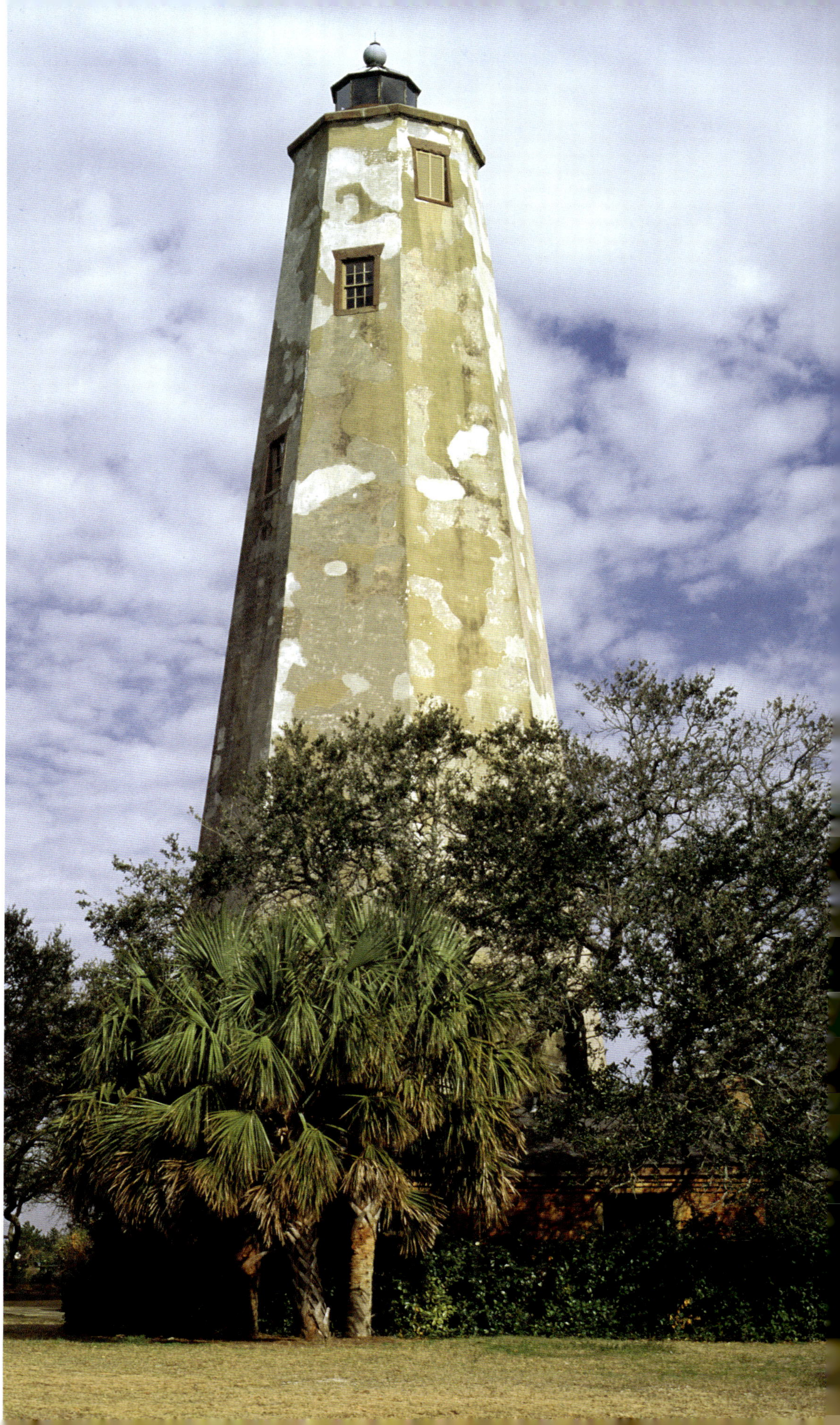

Affectionately referred to by the locals as Old Baldy, the Bald Head Lighthouse is one of nine original lighthouses still standing on North Carolina's shores.

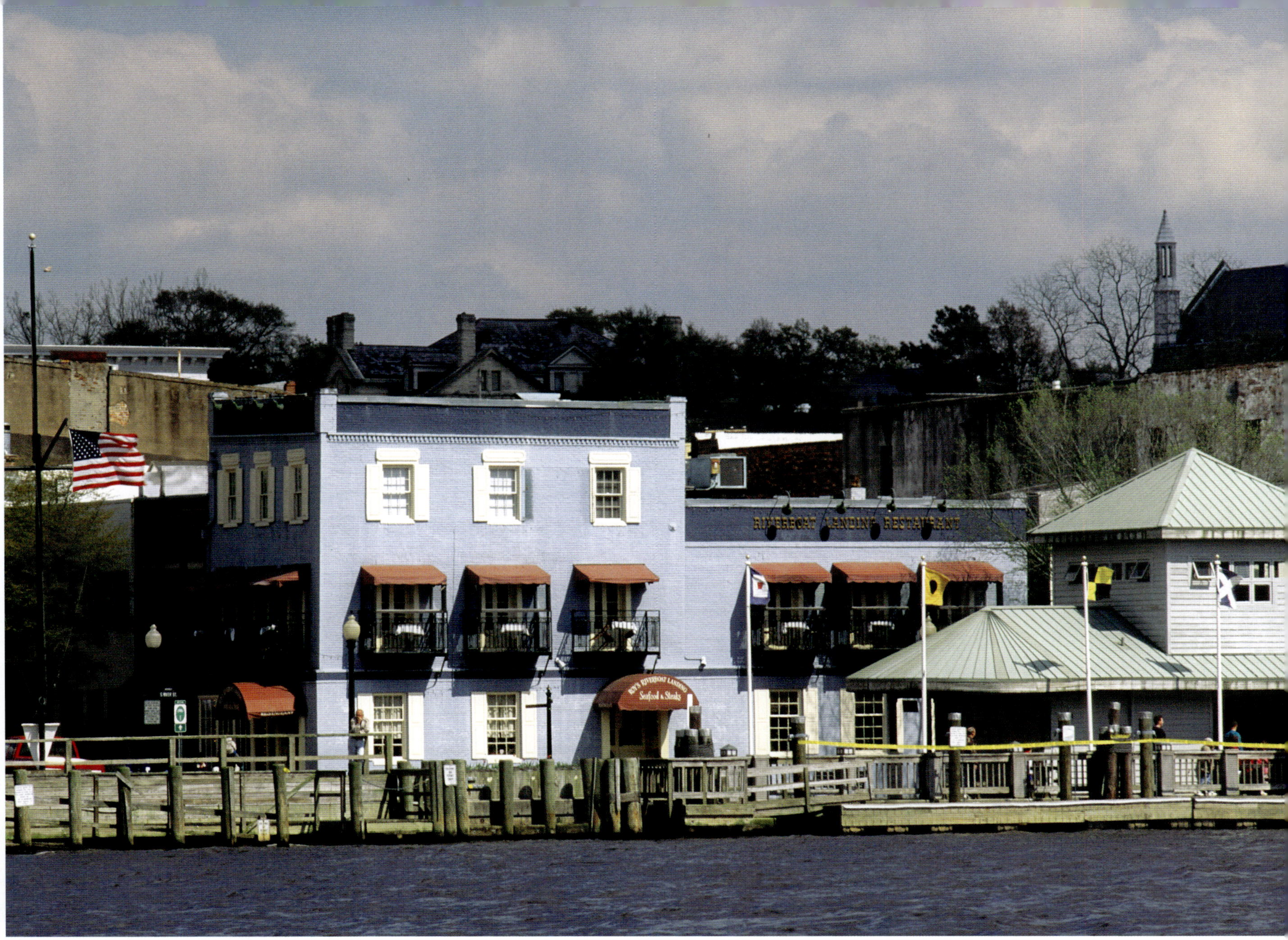

Founded in 1739 in the southeast corner of the state, the port city of Wilmington is rich with history and charm. While grand old homes grace tree-lined boulevards, historic buildings line the waterfront of the Cape Fear River.

FOLLOWING PAGE: The battleship *U.S.S. North Carolina* is now docked in Wilmington, at Eagle's Island. Serving in every major Pacific battle, her primary role was protecting aircraft carriers. The citizens of North Carolina launched a campaign to save the ship as a floating war memorial to the ten thousand North Carolinians who lost their lives fighting for freedom during World War II.

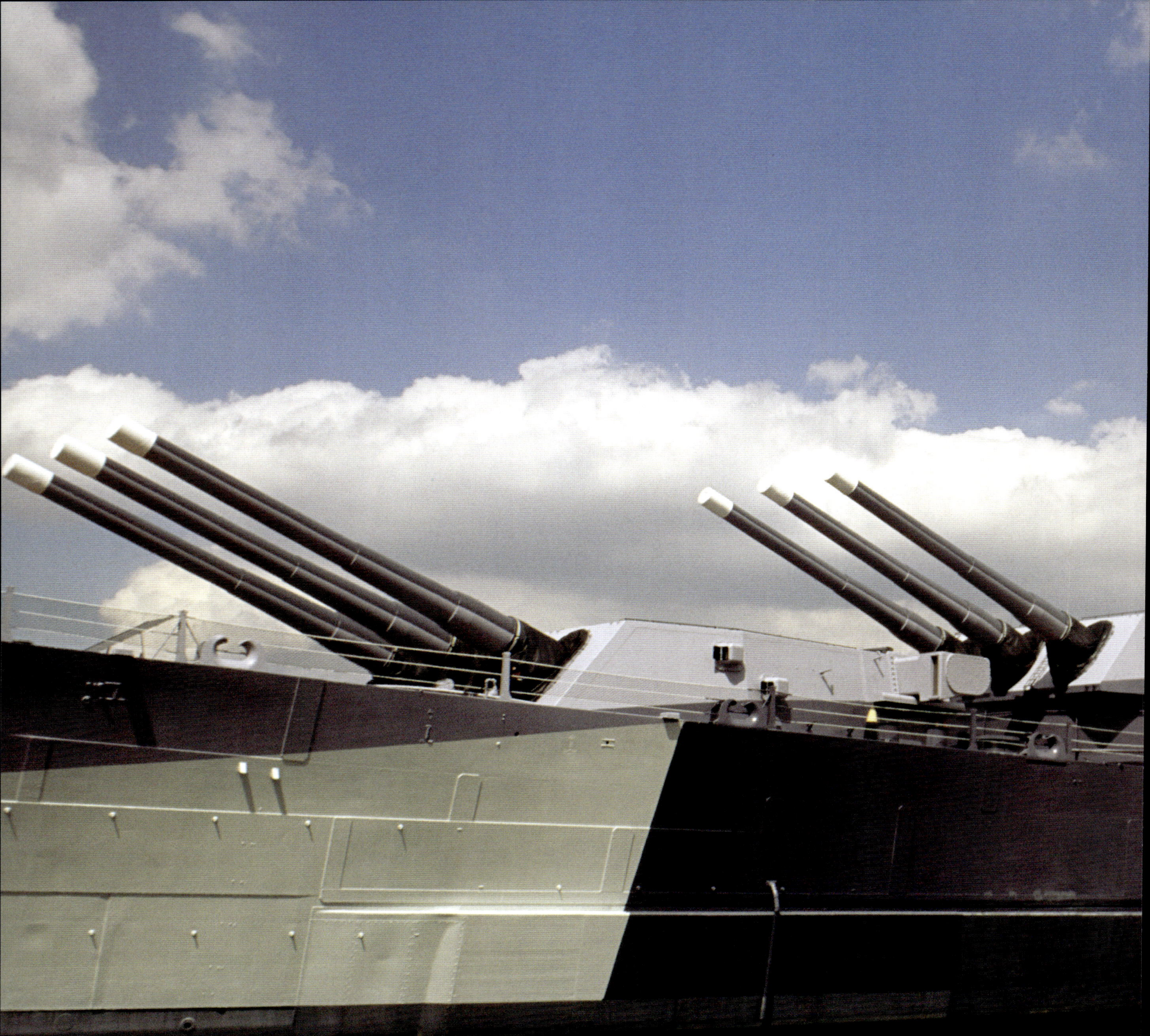

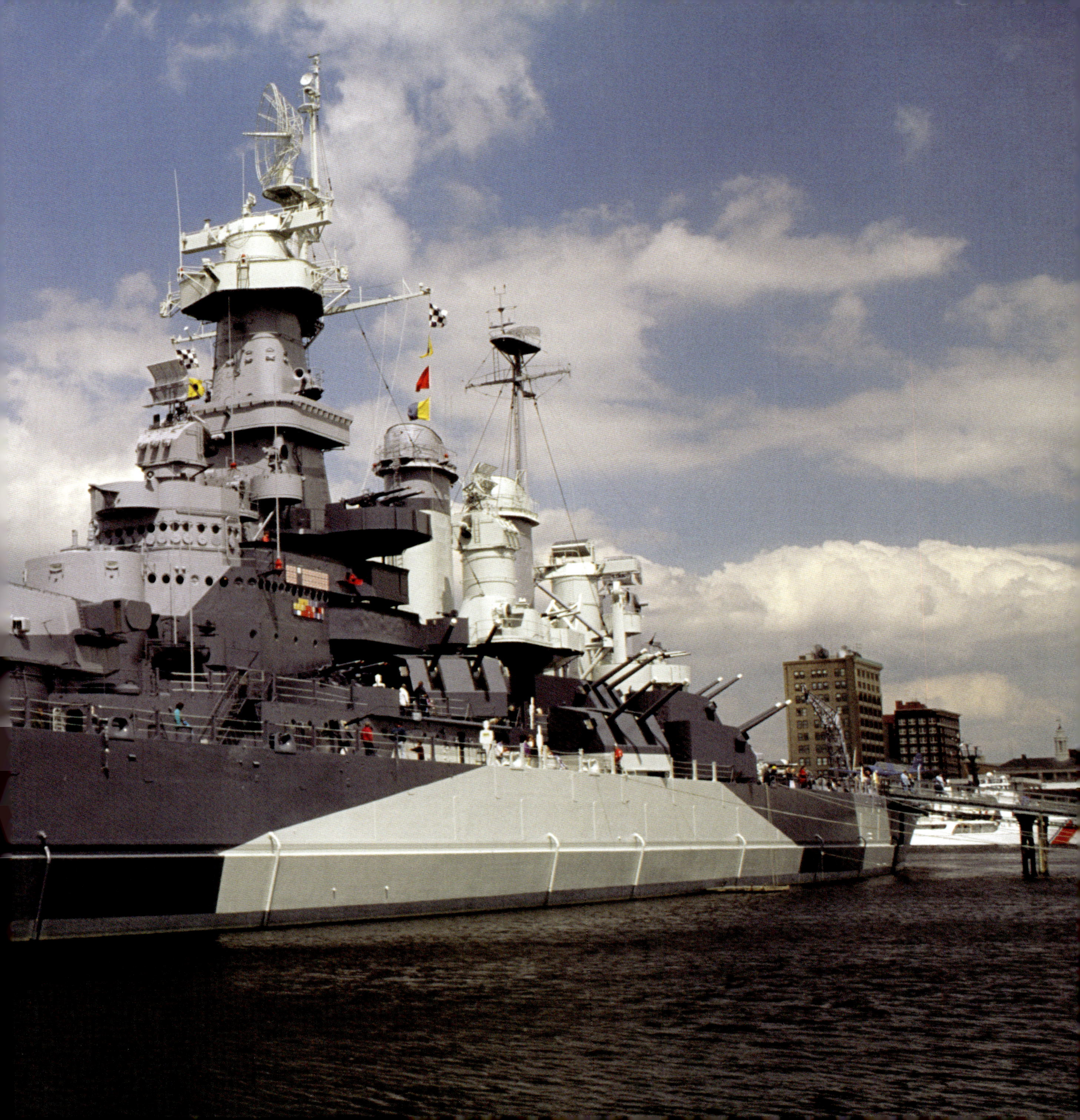

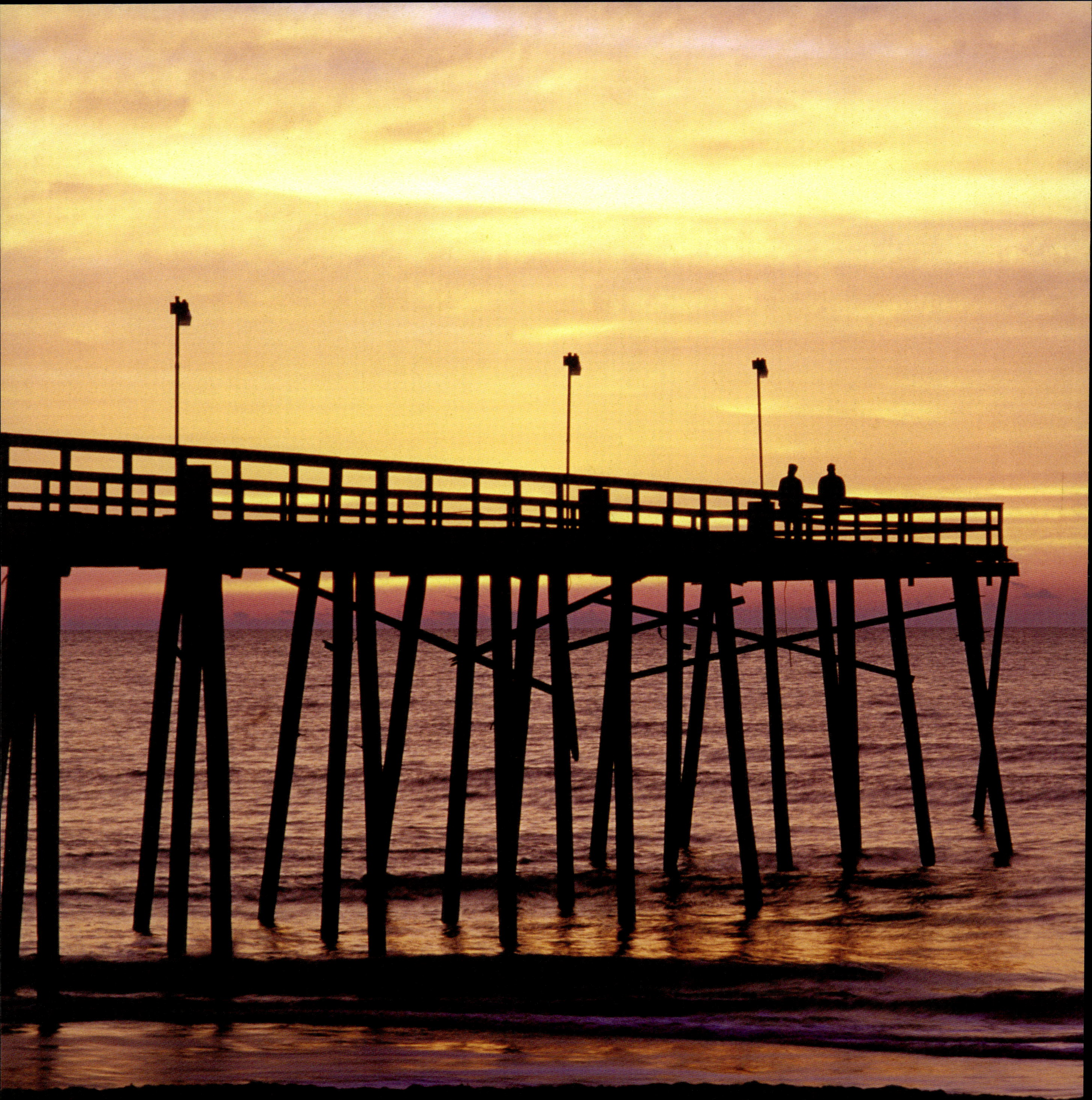

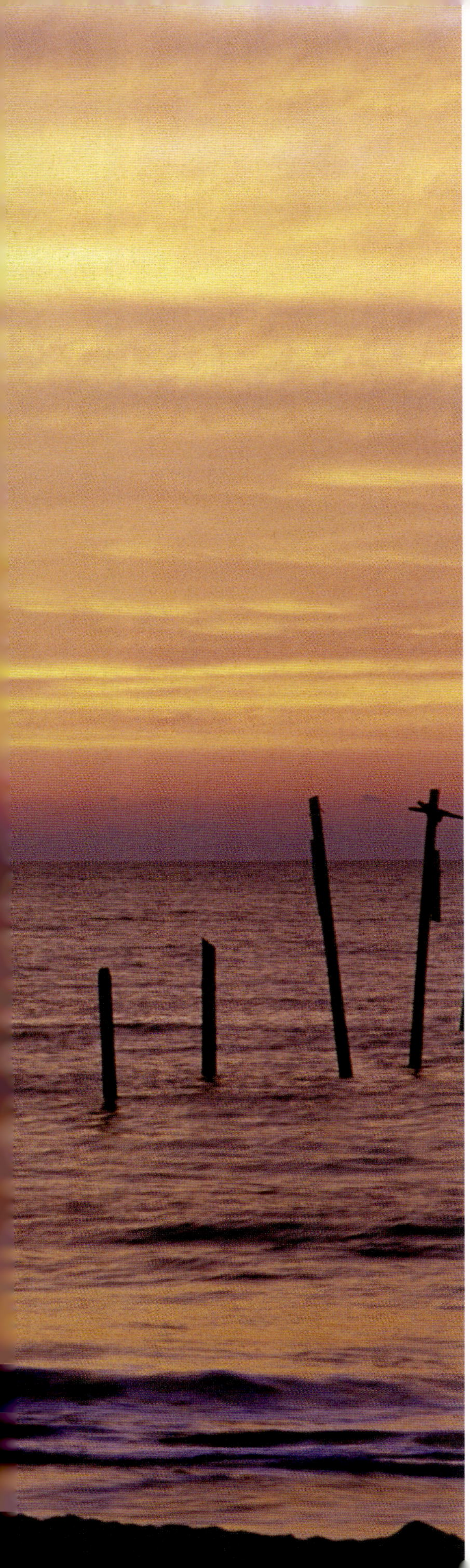

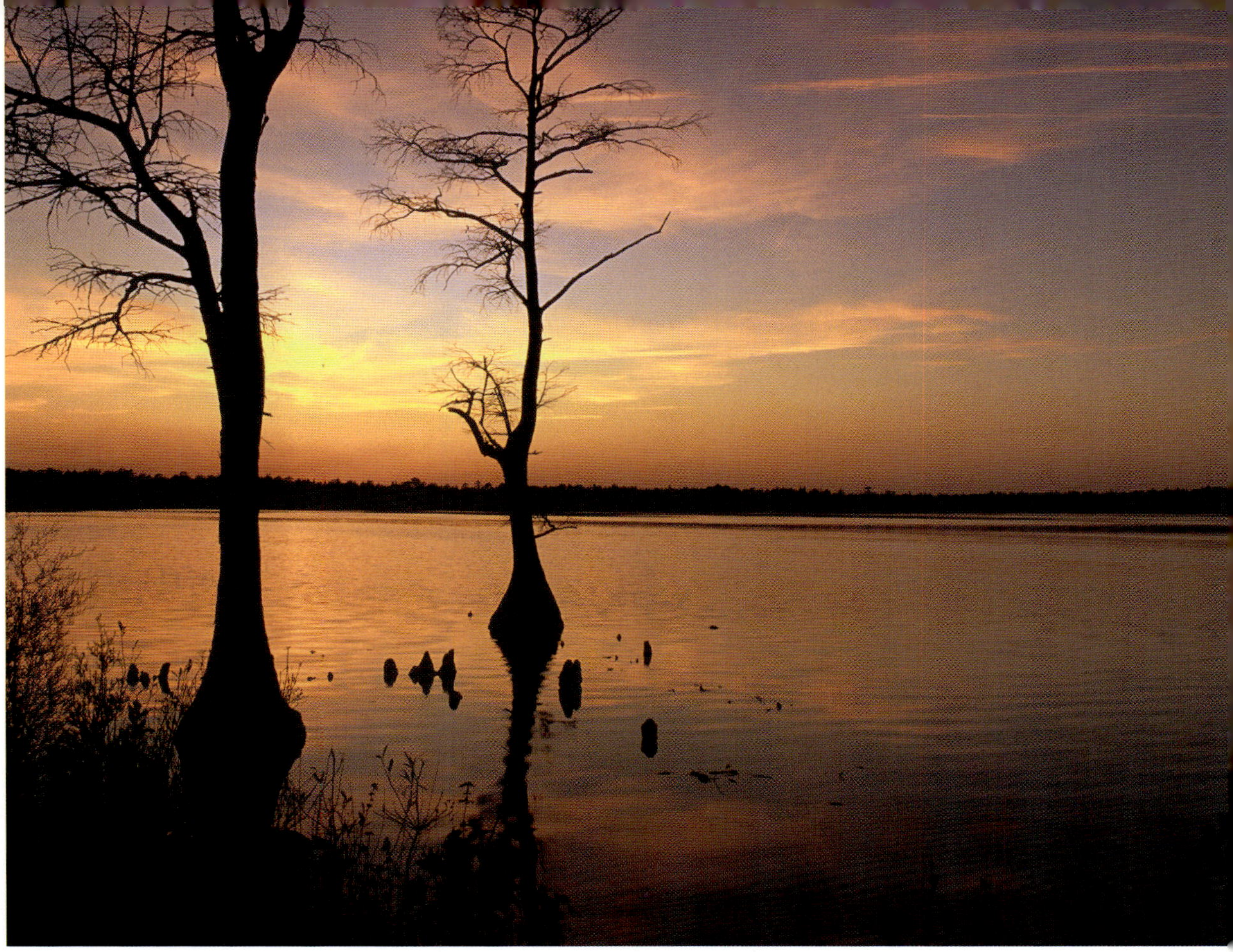

Cypress trees soak their roots in Jones Lake State Park as the sun goes down on the south coast region. Jones Lake opened in 1939 as the first state park for blacks. It later became fully integrated and continues to be a popular recreational destination for swimming and picnicking.

OPPOSITE PAGE: The 750-foot Johnnie Mercer Fishing Pier is a local landmark and a favorite fishing spot. The original wooden pier was rebuilt after Hurricane Fran destroyed it in 1996. It is located on Wrightsville Beach, a beautiful four-mile stretch of sand.

FOLLOWING PAGE: The Intracoastal Waterway is actually a 3,000-mile system of artificial and natural channels and canals along the Atlantic and Gulf coasts. Here, yachts line the calm waters of the Waterway between Wrightsville Beach and Wilmington.

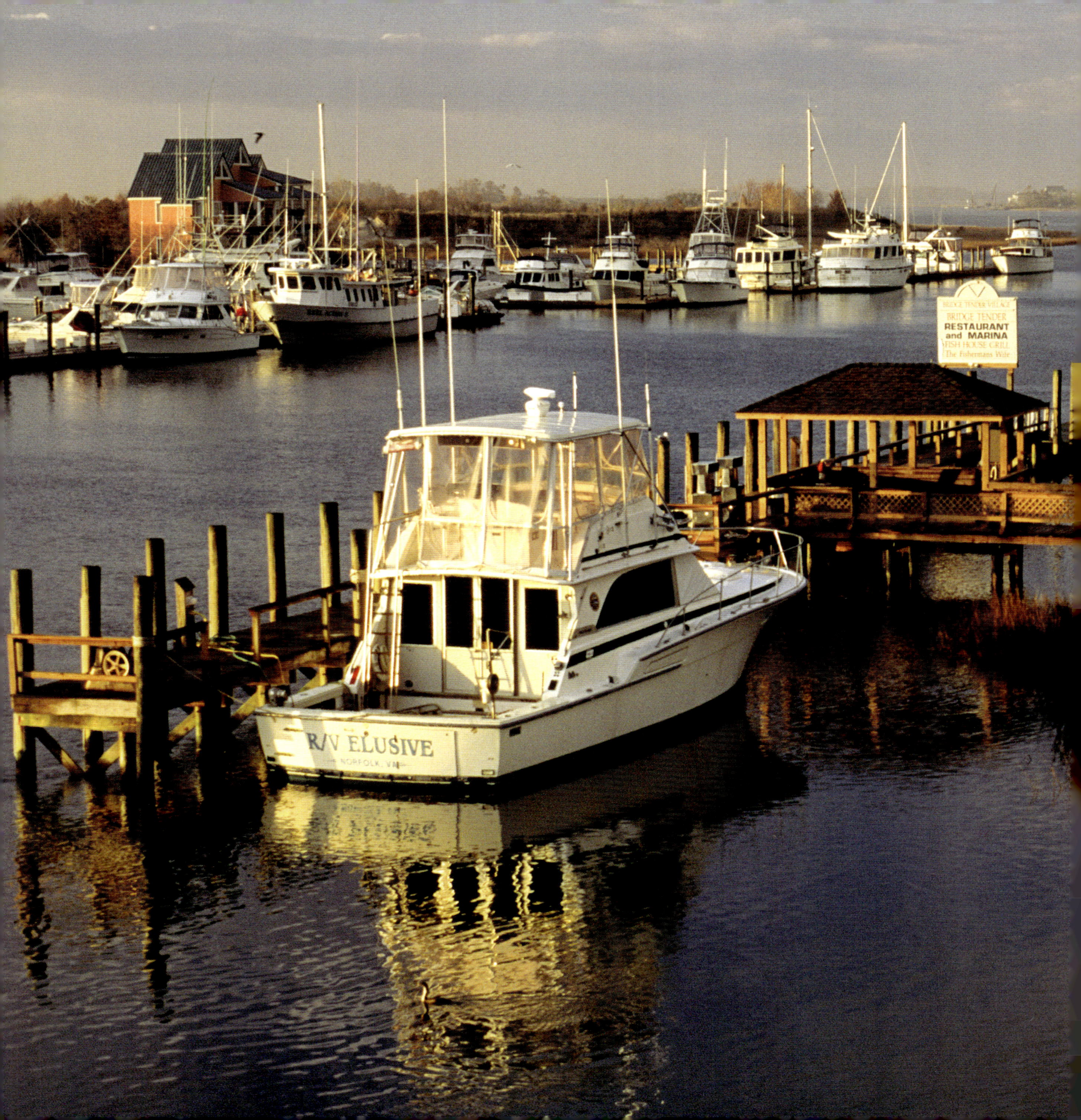
BRIDGE TENDER
RESTAURANT and MARINA
FISH HOUSE GRILL
R/V ELUSIVE
NORFOLK, VA

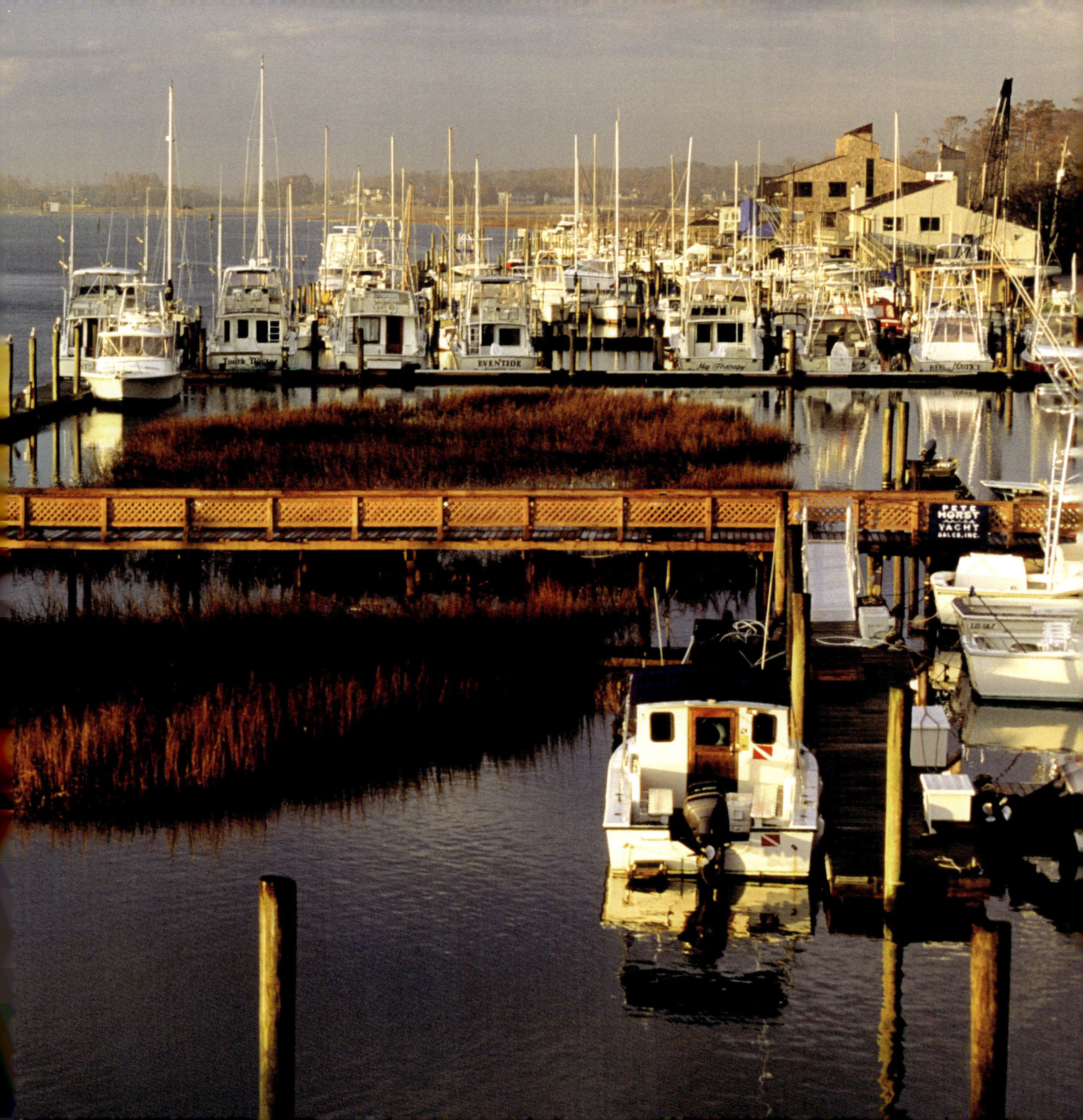
EVENTIDE
PETE HORST
YACHT
SALES, INC.

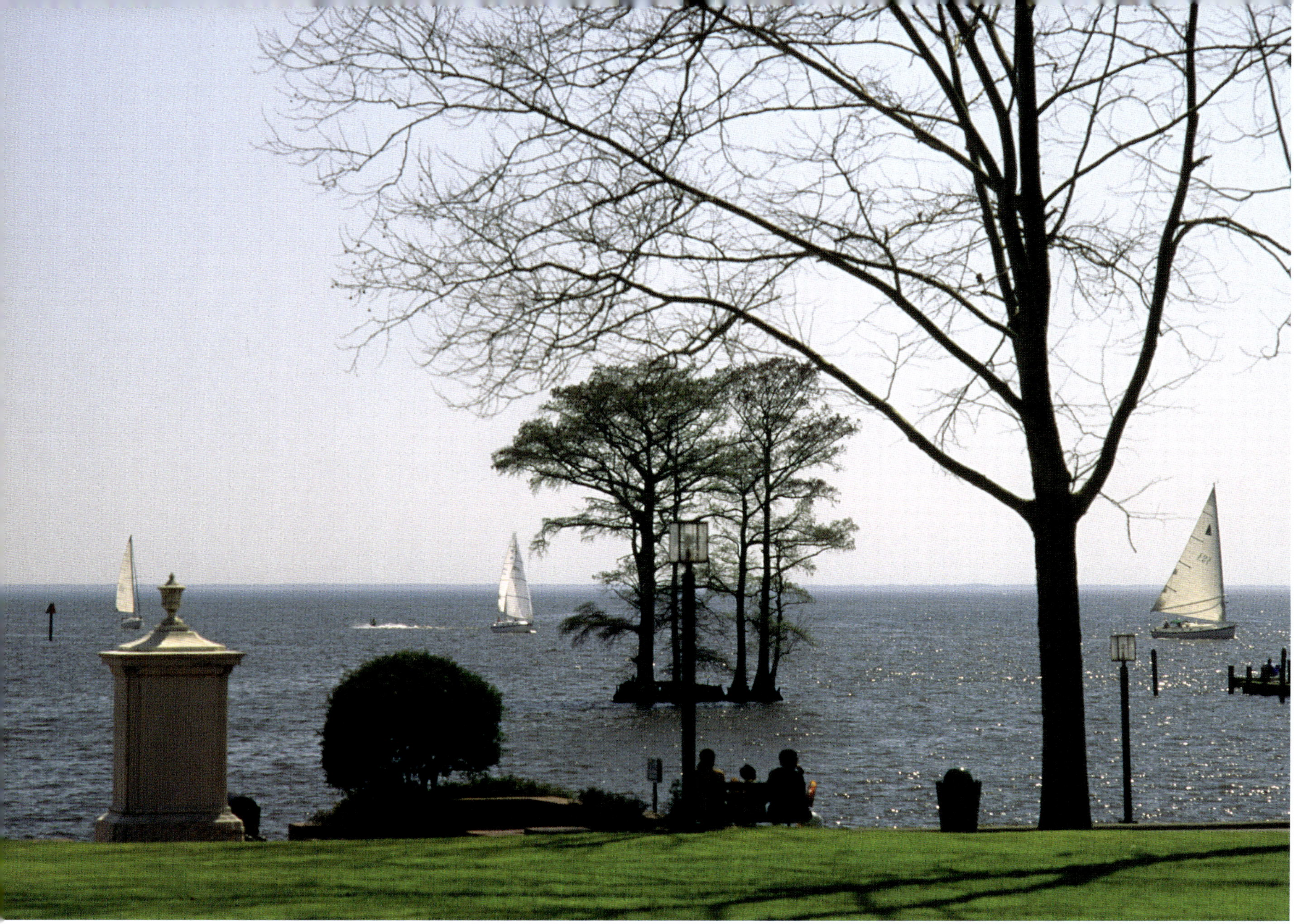

Sailboats dot the waters of the charming colonial town of Edenton Bay on Albemarle Sound in the north coast region. Established in 1712, the town features historic waterfront homes and nearly three centuries of architectural styles.

OPPOSITE PAGE: These surfers enjoy the beach in Salvo, along the Cape Hatteras National Seashore. The Outer Banks is renowned as the best east coast surfing destination, attracting devout surfers from across the globe.

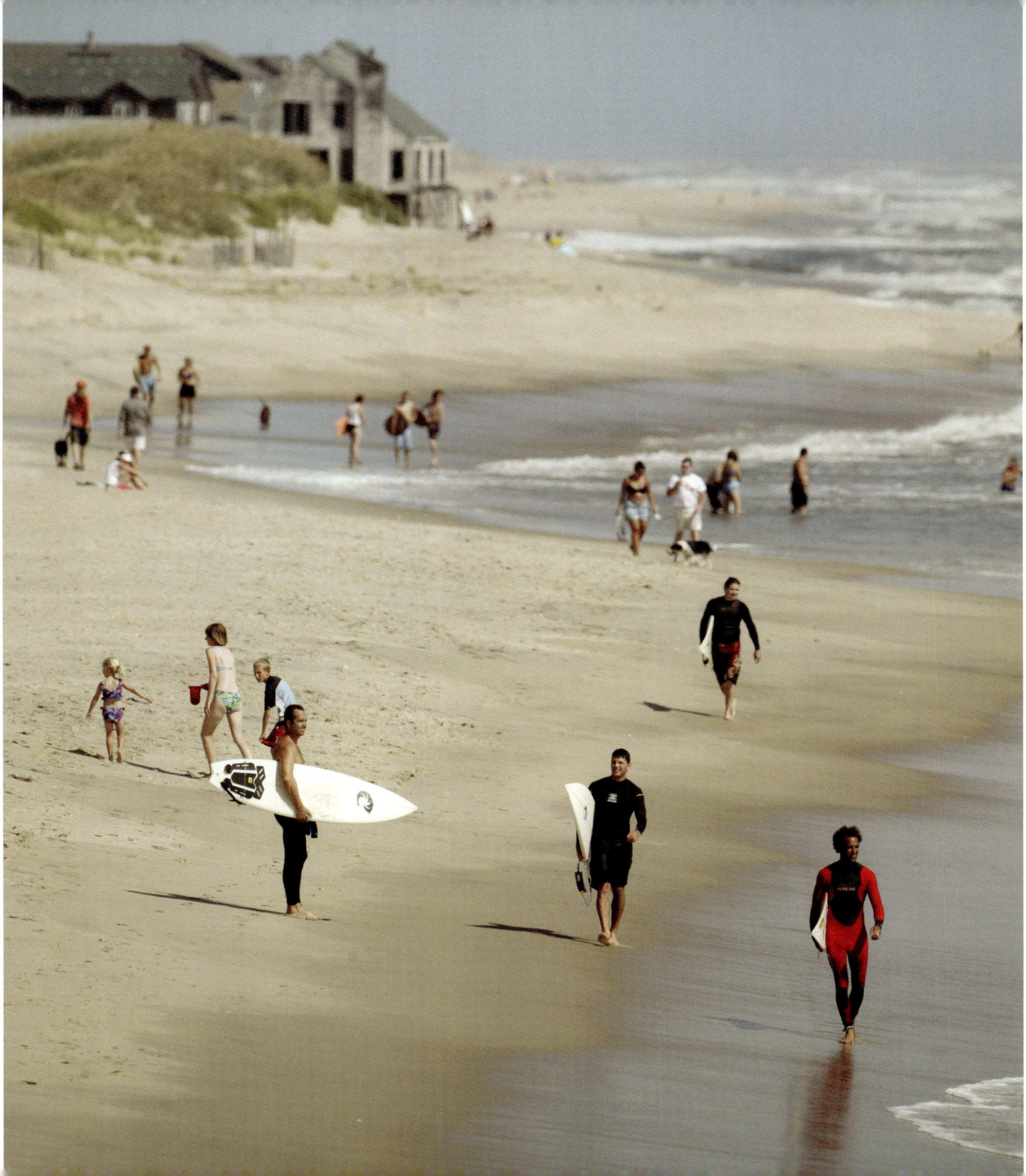

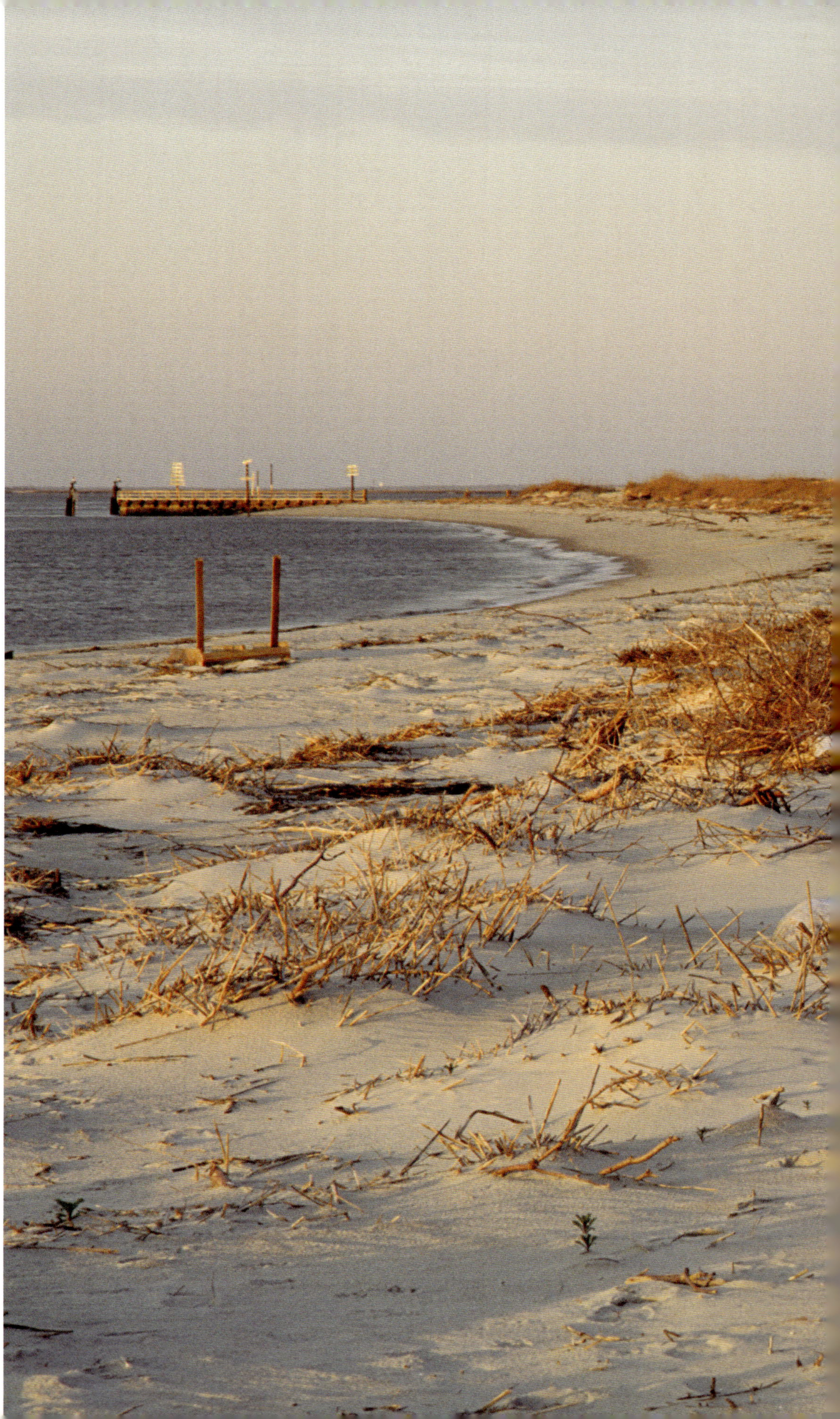

The shadows of the setting sun cool down the soft white sands of West Beach on Bald Head Island in the Outer Banks. Attainable only by boat, Bald Head Island consists of 12,000 acres, of which 10,000 are unspoiled marshes, beaches and maritime forest preserves.

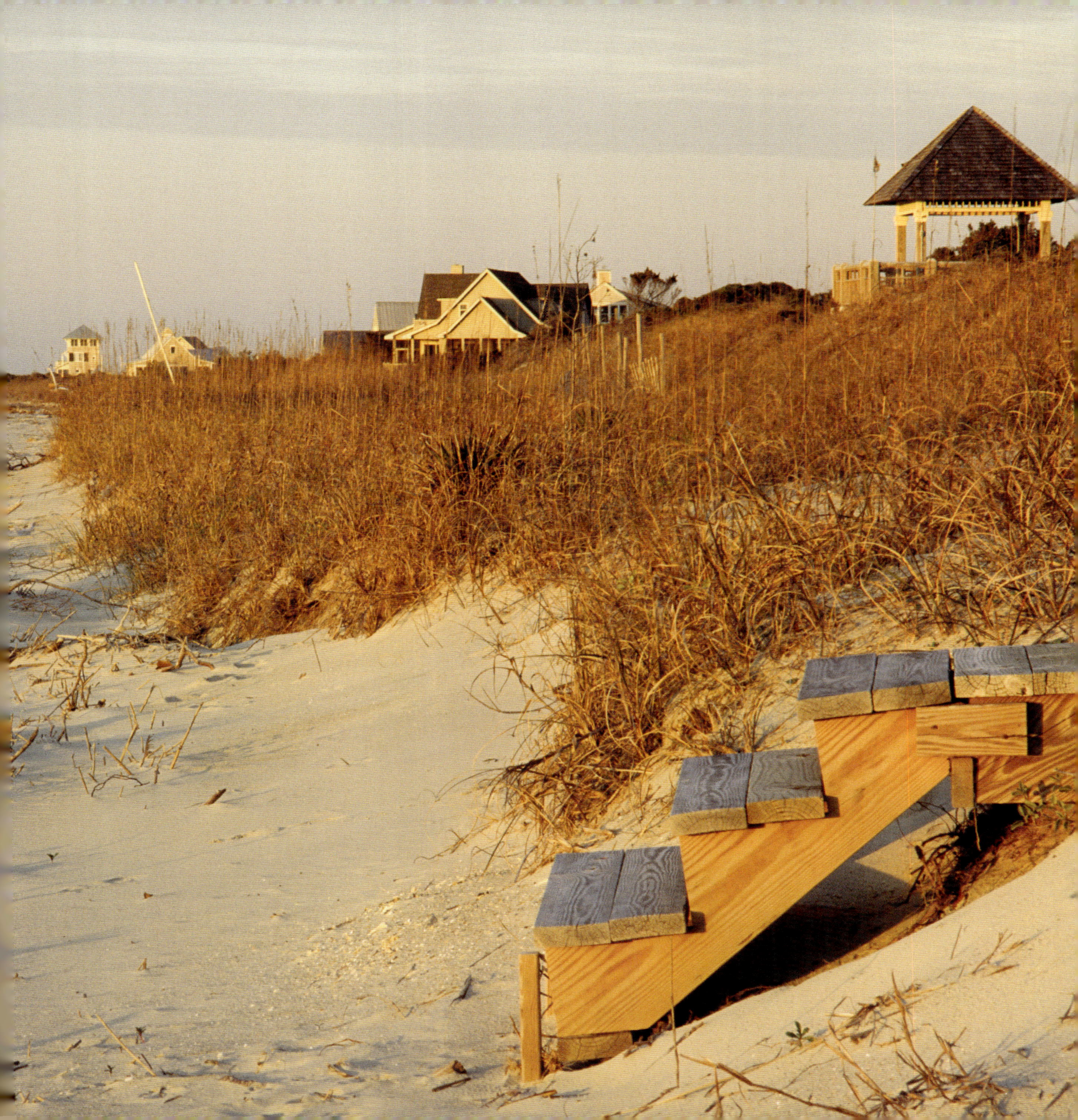